# DIABETIC LIVING® Holiday COOKING VOLUME 9

DIABETIC LIVING® HOLIDAY COOKING
IS PART OF A BOOK SERIES PUBLISHED BY
BETTER HOMES AND GARDENS SPECIAL
INTEREST MEDIA, DES MOINES, IOWA

**Chocolate-Swirled
Pumpkin Bread**
*recipe, p. 115*

**Sweet Potato,
Sausage, and
Goat Cheese
Egg Casserole**
*recipe, p. 9*

## From the Editors

The holiday season means office gatherings, cocktail parties, family get-togethers, and lunches with friends—things that often revolve around food. That can make it easy to indulge a bit more than usual, but you can take control and stay on track with healthy meal planning. Making good food choices is easy when you use recipes from this seasonal collection.

When you're asked to bring a dish to a party, check out Tasty Party Bites, *p. 26*, and choose a dip or appetizer that you can nibble on without worry. Keep a batch of soup or stew *(p. 44)* in the freezer for drop-in visitors. Serve with a plate of carefully curated cookies *(pp. 148–155)*. Turn to Main-Dish Masterpieces, *p. 60*, for a grand dinner with breads or rolls *(p. 112)* and side dishes *(p. 92)* that are deliciously good for you.

The recipes in this book were developed with great taste as a priority. But you can count on them to have just-right portions and sensible carb, calorie, and sodium amounts to make healthful meal planning easy at this busy time. Whether you need dinner for a crowd or an easy weeknight meal, you'll be ready.

### On the Cover:

*(clockwise from top left)* **Chocolate Snowball Cookies**, *p. 151*, **Chai-Spiced Pine Cones**, *p. 155*, **Sugar Cookie Cutouts**, *p. 148*, **Pistachio-Cranberry Sticks**, *p. 155*, **Mint-Ganach Sandwich Cookies**, *p.155*, **Almond Spirals**, *p. 150*

Photographer: Jason Donnelly
Food Stylist: Sammy Mila

**78**

**120**

**138**

DIABETIC LIVING® Holiday COOKING VOLUME 9

### CONSUMER MARKETING

| | |
|---|---|
| Vice President, Consumer Marketing | STEVE CROWE |
| Consumer Marketing Product Director | HEATHER SORENSEN |
| Consumer Marketing Billing/Renewal Manager | TAMI PERKINS |
| Consumer Marketing Product Manager | WENDY MERICAL |
| Business Director | DIANE UMLAND |
| Production Manager | AL RODRUCK |
| Contributing Project Manager | SHELLI MCCONNELL, PURPLE PEAR PUBLISHING, INC. |
| Contributing Photographer | JASON DONNELLY |
| Contributing Food Stylist | SAMMY MILA |
| Test Kitchen Director | LYNN BLANCHARD |
| Test Kitchen Chef | CARLA CHRISTIAN, RD, LD |

### DIABETIC LIVING® MAGAZINE

| | |
|---|---|
| Editorial DIrector | JESSIE PRICE |
| Executive Editor | LAUREN LASTOWKA |
| Creative Director | JAMES VAN FLETEREN |
| Associate Editor | MICAELA YOUNG, M.S. |
| Managing Editor | WENDY S. RUOPP, M.S. |

### MEREDITH NATIONAL MEDIA GROUP

President JON WERTHER

Chairman and Chief Executive Officer STEPHEN M. LACY

Vice Chairman MELL MEREDITH FRAZIER

In Memoriam— E.T. MEREDITH III (1933–2003)

Diabetic Living® Holiday Cooking is part of a series published by Meredith Corp., 1716 Locust St., Des Moines, IA 50309-3023.

If you have comments or questions about the editorial material in *Diabetic Living® Holiday Cooking,* write to the editor of *Diabetic Living* magazine, Meredith Corp., 1716 Locust St., Des Moines, IA 50309-3023. Send an e-mail to *diabeticlivingmeredith.com* or call 800/678-2651. *Diabetic Living®* magazine is available by subscription or on the newsstand. To order a subscription to the magazine, go to *DiabeticLivingOnline.com*

# CONTENTS

# 1

# EYE-OPENING
# **BREAKFASTS**

Holiday time calls for a variety of breakfast options. Most day-to-day routines don't stop, so you'll find quick, wholesome choices to keep you on track with your meal plans. Look for brunch recipes such as egg casserole, breakfast tart, and eggs Benedict that are company-special and satisfying for everyone.

Chocolate-Swirled
Pumpkin Bread
*recipe, p. 115*

Sweet Potato,
Sausage, and
Goat Cheese
Egg Casserole

## Sweet Potato, Sausage, and Goat Cheese Egg Casserole

**12 g CARB**

**SERVES** 8
**HANDS ON** 30 min.
**TOTAL** 1 hr. 20 min.

Nonstick cooking spray
6 oz. lean turkey breakfast sausage
1 tsp. olive oil
1 cup chopped onion
1 cup chopped red or green sweet pepper
4 cloves garlic, minced
1 Tbsp. water
1 5-oz. pkg. fresh baby spinach
1½ cups roasted sweet potatoes (from Sweet Potato and Wild Rice Dressing, *p. 101*)
8 eggs, lightly beaten
4 egg whites
½ cup low-fat (1%) milk
½ tsp. dry mustard
½ tsp. crushed red pepper
½ tsp. black pepper
⅛ tsp. salt
½ cup crumbled goat cheese (chèvre) (2 oz.)
2 Tbsp. chopped green onion

**1.** Preheat oven to 350°F. Coat a 4-qt. baking dish with cooking spray.
**2.** In a 10-inch nonstick skillet cook sausage over medium 5 to 7 minutes or until browned, breaking up meat as it cooks. Remove from skillet; drain off fat.
**3.** In the same skillet heat oil over medium high. Add onion, sweet pepper, and garlic; cook 6 to 8 minutes or until tender, stirring occasionally. Add the water, stirring to scrape up any browned bits. Add spinach; cook about 2 minutes or until wilted. Stir in cooked sausage and sweet potatoes. Transfer mixture to the prepared baking dish.

**4.** In a bowl combine the next seven ingredients (through salt). Pour over sausage mixture.
**5.** Bake 35 to 40 minutes or until center is set (160°F). Top with cheese and green onion. Let stand 15 minutes before serving.

**PER SERVING** (¾ cup each) **CAL** 219, **FAT** 11 g (4 g sat. fat), **CHOL** 215 mg, **SODIUM** 446 mg, **CARB** 12 g (2 g fiber, 4 g sugars), **PRO** 17 g

 **QUICK TIP** If you aren't planning to make the Sweet Potato and Wild Rice Dressing, then toss 2 cups cubed sweet potatoes in 1 Tbsp. olive oil and ¼ tsp. each salt and black pepper. Place in a 15×10-inch baking pan and roast in a 450°F oven about 25 minutes or until tender and browned.

Feta-Radish
Quiche

## Feta-Radish Quiche

**15 g**
**CARB**

**SERVES** 8
**HANDS ON** 25 min.
**TOTAL** 1 hr. 15 min.

½ of a 14.1-oz. pkg. (1 crust) rolled
   refrigerated unbaked piecrust
6 oz. assorted radishes, trimmed
   and thinly sliced
3 eggs, lightly beaten
3 egg whites
1¼ cups milk
½ cup crumbled feta cheese
   (2 oz.)
1 Tbsp. snipped fresh dill
¼ tsp. salt
⅛ tsp. black pepper

**1.** Preheat oven to 450°F. Let piecrust
stand according to package
directions. Unroll piecrust and fit into
a 9-inch pie plate. Fold under extra
dough; crimp edge as desired. Do
not prick piecrust. Line piecrust with
a double thickness of foil. Bake
8 minutes; remove foil. Bake about

4 minutes more or until set and dry.
Remove from oven.
**2.** Reduce oven temperature to 350°F.
Arrange radishes in a circular pattern
on bottom of partially baked piecrust.
In a bowl combine the remaining
ingredients. Pour over radishes.
**3.** Bake 40 to 45 minutes or until a
knife comes out clean. Transfer to a
wire rack. Let stand 10 minutes before
serving. If desired, top with additional
fresh dill.

**PER SERVING** *(1 wedge each)* **CAL** 174,
**FAT** 10 g (5 g sat. fat), **CHOL** 82 mg,
**SODIUM** 341 mg, **CARB** 15 g (0 g fiber,
3 g sugars), **PRO** 7 g

**Tip** To thinly slice radishes, use a
mandoline or a chef's knife to cut slices
about ⅛ inch thick.

## Rainbow Frittata

**9 g**
**CARB**

**SERVES** 4
**TOTAL** 30 min.

Nonstick cooking spray
¼ cup ½-inch pieces orange
   sweet pepper
¼ cup ½-inch pieces yellow
   sweet pepper
¼ cup coarsely chopped
   fresh broccoli
8 eggs
1 tsp. snipped fresh basil
½ tsp. snipped fresh thyme
⅛ tsp. salt
⅛ tsp. cracked black pepper
1 avocado, halved, seeded,
   peeled, and thinly sliced
1½ cups grape or cherry tomatoes,
   halved
   Sriracha sauce

**1.** Preheat oven to 350 F. Coat an
oven-going 10-inch nonstick skillet
with cooking spray. Add sweet
peppers and broccoli; cook and
stir over medium 5 to 7 minutes or
until tender.
**2.** In a bowl whisk together eggs,
basil, thyme, salt, and black pepper.
Pour over vegetables in skillet. Cook,
without stirring, until mixture begins
to set on bottom and around edges.
Using a spatula, lift egg mixture so
uncooked portion flows underneath.
**3.** Transfer skillet to oven; bake about
5 minutes or until egg mixture is set.
Remove from oven. Let stand
2 minutes. Top with avocado and
tomatoes. Drizzle with sriracha sauce.

**PER SERVING** *(¼ frittata + ¾ cup tomato
mixture each)* **CAL** 225, **FAT** 15 g (4 g sat. fat),
**CHOL** 372 mg, **SODIUM** 236 mg, **CARB** 9 g
(4 g fiber, 3 g sugars), **PRO** 14 g

**Rainbow Frittata**

Breakfast Stuffed Peppers

## Breakfast Skillet Hash

**23 g**
**CARB**

**SERVES** 4
**TOTAL** 40 min.

- 2 Tbsp. olive oil
- 1 large sweet potato (12 oz.), peeled and cut into ¾-inch pieces
- ½ cup chopped onion
- ½ cup refrigerated cooked crumbled turkey sausage
- 1½ cups refrigerated or frozen egg product, thawed
- ½ tsp. dried Italian seasoning, crushed
- ¼ tsp. garlic powder
- ¼ tsp. black pepper
- ⅛ tsp. salt
- 2 cups fresh baby spinach
- ½ cup shredded reduced-fat Italian four cheese blend (2 oz.)

**1.** Heat a 10-inch cast-iron skillet over medium about 5 minutes or until very hot. Add oil to skillet. Add sweet potato; cook 15 minutes, stirring occasionally. Add onion and sausage. Cook about 5 minutes more or until vegetables are tender, stirring frequently.

**2.** Add the next five ingredients (through salt). Cook, without stirring, until mixture begins to set on bottom and around edges. Using a spatula or large spoon, lift and fold partially cooked egg mixture so uncooked portion flows underneath. Continue cooking 2 to 3 minutes or until egg mixture is cooked through but is still glossy and moist. Gradually add spinach, tossing just until wilted. Sprinkle with cheese.

**PER SERVING** (¾ cup each) **CAL** 256, **FAT** 10 g (3 g sat. fat), **CHOL** 18 mg, **SODIUM** 545 mg, **CARB** 23 g (4 g fiber, 5 g sugars), **PRO** 18 g

## Breakfast Stuffed Peppers

**36 g**
**CARB**

**SERVES** 4
**HANDS ON** 20 min.
**TOTAL** 1 hr. 5 min.

- 2 extra-large red or green sweet peppers
- 1⅓ cups cooked brown rice
- 1 cup canned reduced-sodium black beans, rinsed and drained
- 1 cup seeded and chopped tomato
- ½ cup shredded Mexican cheese blend or cheddar cheese (2 oz.)
- 1 tsp. salt-free Southwest chipotle or fiesta lime seasoning
- ½ tsp. salt
- 1 cup water
- 4 eggs
  Snipped fresh cilantro (optional)

**1.** Preheat oven to 350°F. Halve sweet peppers lengthwise; remove seeds and membranes.

**2.** For filling, in a bowl combine rice, beans, tomato, ¼ cup of the cheese, the Southwest seasoning, and salt. Spoon filling into pepper halves. Using the back of a spoon, make an indentation in filling. Place in a 2-qt. square baking dish. Pour the water into dish around pepper halves.

**3.** Bake, covered, 30 minutes. Remove from oven. Break an egg into a custard cup and slip into an indentation in filling. Repeat with remaining eggs. Bake, covered, about 15 minutes more or until egg whites are completely set or to desired doneness. Sprinkle with remaining ¼ cup cheese and, if desired, cilantro.

**PER SERVING** (1 stuffed pepper half each) **CAL** 298, **FAT** 10 g (4 g sat. fat), **CHOL** 199 mg, **SODIUM** 538 mg, **CARB** 36 g (6 g fiber, 6 g sugars), **PRO** 16 g

Breakfast Skillet Hash

# Savory Tomato-Mozzarella Tart

**17 g**
CARB

**SERVES** 8
**HANDS ON** 30 min.
**TOTAL** 1 hr.

½ of a 14.1-oz. pkg. (1 crust) rolled refrigerated unbaked piecrust
4 eggs, lightly beaten
1¼ cups low-fat (1%) milk
1 cup chopped green onions
¾ cup shredded part-skim mozzarella cheese (3 oz.)
2 Tbsp. snipped fresh basil or 1 tsp. dried basil, crushed
¼ to ½ tsp. salt
¼ tsp. black pepper
½ cup chopped oil-packed dried tomatoes

**1.** Preheat oven to 450°F. Let piecrust stand according to package directions. On a lightly floured surface roll pastry into a 13-inch circle. Transfer to a 9-inch pie plate. Trim to ½ inch beyond edge of plate; crimp edge. Do not prick pastry. Line pastry with a double thickness of foil. Bake 12 minutes; remove foil. Cool on a wire rack. Reduce oven temperature to 325°F.

**2.** For filling, in a large bowl combine eggs and milk. Stir in next five ingredients (through black pepper). Pour into partially baked pastry shell; sprinkle with tomatoes.

**3.** Bake 40 to 45 minutes or until a knife comes out clean. Let stand 15 minutes before serving. If desired, top with additional fresh basil.

PER SERVING *(1 wedge each)* **CAL** 197, **FAT** 11 g (5 g sat. fat), **CHOL** 104 mg, **SODIUM** 340 mg, **CARB** 17 g (1 g fiber, 2 g sugars), **PRO** 8 g

Portobello Spinach
Eggs Benedict

1. Sprinkle mushroom caps with the salt and pepper. In a 10-inch skillet heat 2 tsp. of the oil over medium. Cook mushroom caps in hot oil 8 to 10 minutes or until tender, turning once. Transfer caps to a plate; cover with foil.

2. Meanwhile, for sauce, in a bowl whisk together the next six ingredients (through hot sauce) until smooth.

3. Heat the remaining 2 tsp. oil in skillet over medium. Add garlic; cook and stir 1 minute. Add spinach, broth, and Cajun seasoning; cook and stir about 1 minute until spinach is just wilted. Keep warm. Wipe skillet clean.

4. To poach eggs, fill the skillet halfway with water. Bring water to boiling; reduce heat to simmering (bubbles should begin to break the surface of the water). Break one of the eggs Into a custard cup. Carefully slide egg into simmering water, holding the lip of the cup as close to the water as possible. Repeat with the remaining eggs, positioning so the eggs don't touch. Simmer, uncovered, 3 to 5 minutes or until egg whites are completely set and yolks begin to thicken but are not hard. Remove eggs from pan with a slotted spoon; blot on a paper towel to remove excess water.

5. Top mushroom caps with spinach mixture, poached eggs, and sauce. If desired, sprinkle with additional Cajun seasoning.

**PER SERVING** *(1 mushroom cap + 1 egg + 1 Tbsp. sauce each)* **CAL** 167, **FAT** 11 g (3 g sat. fat), **CHOL** 188 mg, **SODIUM** 383 mg, **CARB** 7 g (2 g fiber, 3 g sugars), **PRO** 10 g

## Portobello Spinach Eggs Benedict

**7g**
**CARB**

**SERVES** 4
**HANDS ON** 15 min.
**TOTAL** 30 min.

- 4 small fresh portobello mushrooms (about 3 oz. each), stems and gills removed
- ¼ tsp. salt
- ¼ tsp. black pepper
- 4 tsp. olive oil
- 2 Tbsp. plain fat-free yogurt or fat-free sour cream
- 4 tsp. light mayonnaise
- 2 tsp. Dijon mustard
- 2 tsp. lemon juice
- 2 tsp. snipped fresh tarragon or thyme
- 10 to 12 drops hot pepper sauce
- 4 cloves garlic, minced
- 4 cups fresh spinach, chopped
- ¼ cup reduced-sodium chicken broth or vegetable broth
- ½ tsp. salt-free Cajun seasoning or seafood seasoning
- 4 eggs

Shakshuka

## Shakshuka

**29 g** CARB

**SERVES** 4
**TOTAL** 30 min.

2 Tbsp. olive oil
3 cloves garlic, minced
6 ripe medium tomatoes (about 2 lb.), peeled and coarsely chopped
½ tsp. salt
¼ tsp. crushed red pepper
¼ tsp. black pepper
4 eggs
2 Tbsp. snipped fresh basil or oregano

4 wedges Italian flatbread (focaccia)

**1.** For sauce, in a 10-inch skillet heat 1 Tbsp. of the oil over medium. Add garlic; cook and stir 1 minute. Stir in tomatoes, salt, crushed red pepper, and black pepper. Bring to boiling; reduce heat. Boil gently, uncovered, 12 to 15 minutes or until tomato juice begins to thicken, stirring and crushing tomatoes occasionally with the back of a spoon.
**2.** Crack an egg into a custard cup; slip egg into sauce. Repeat with remaining eggs. Reduce heat. Simmer,

covered, about 5 minutes or until egg whites are set and yolks are thickened.
**3.** Drizzle eggs with remaining 1 Tbsp. oil before serving and sprinkle with basil. Serve with flatbread.

PER SERVING (1 egg + ⅔ cup mixture each) CAL 310, FAT 16 g (3 g sat. fat), CHOL 186 mg, SODIUM 691 mg, CARB 29 g (3 g fiber, 6 g sugars), PRO 13 g

## Blueberry-Ricotta Pancakes

**17 g**
**CARB**

**SERVES** 8
**HANDS ON** 25 min.
**TOTAL** 35 min.

- ½ cup all-purpose flour
- 2 tsp. baking powder
- ½ tsp. salt
- 1 cup ricotta cheese
- 4 egg yolks
- 3 Tbsp. sugar*
- ¼ cup milk
- 1½ cups fresh or frozen blueberries
- 4 egg whites
- 1 recipe Blueberry Syrup (optional)

**1.** In a large bowl combine flour, baking powder, and salt. In a medium bowl whisk together ricotta cheese, egg yolks, and sugar until well mixed. Add ricotta mixture to flour mixture; stir until smooth. Stir in milk. Fold in blueberries.

**2.** In a small bowl beat egg whites with a mixer on high until stiff peaks form (tips stand straight). Gently fold beaten egg whites into batter, leaving a few puffs of egg white. Do not overbeat.

**3.** For each pancake, pour about ¼ cup of the batter onto a hot, lightly greased griddle or heavy skillet. Spread batter into a circle about 4 inches in diameter. Cook over medium 1 to 2 minutes per side or until pancakes are golden brown, turning to second sides when surfaces are bubbly and edges are slightly dry. Serve immediately or keep warm in a loosely covered baking dish in a 300°F oven. If desired, serve with Blueberry Syrup.

**PER SERVING** *(2 pancakes each)* **CAL** 156, **FAT** 7 g (3 g sat. fat), **CHOL** 109 mg, **SODIUM** 329 mg, **CARB** 17 g (1 g fiber, 8 g sugars), **PRO** 8 g

***Sugar Sub** Choose Splenda Sugar Blend. Follow package directions to use 3 Tbsp. equivalent.

**PER SERVING WITH SUB** Same as original, except **CAL** 149, **CARB** 14 g (6 g sugars)

**Blueberry Syrup** In a 2-qt. saucepan combine **2 cups fresh or frozen blueberries, 1 cup pure maple syrup,** and **2 tsp. lime or lemon juice**. Bring to boiling; reduce heat. Simmer, uncovered, 15 to 20 minutes or until blueberries become soft, stirring occasionally. Thoroughly mash blueberries. Strain blueberry mixture through a fine-mesh sieve or a strainer lined with 100%-cotton cheesecloth set over a medium bowl. Discard solids. Serve warm. To store, pour syrup into an airtight storage container; cover. Store in the refrigerator up to 1 week.

**QUICK TIP** Use this fruit syrup to drizzle over pancakes, waffles, yogurt, ice cream, and more.

**Blueberry-Ricotta Pancakes**

## Overnight Lemon-Cream French Toast Cups

**34 g**
**CARB**

| | |
|---|---|
| **SERVES** 6 | |
| **HANDS ON** 30 min. | |
| **TOTAL** 8 hr. 50 min. | |

Nonstick cooking spray

4 cups dry whole grain or challah bread cubes

1 large lemon

4 oz. reduced-fat cream cheese (neufchatel), softened

¼ cup honey

¾ cup refrigerated or frozen egg product, thawed, or 3 eggs, lightly beaten

¼ cup fat-free milk

2 cups coarsely chopped fresh strawberries

1 tsp. honey

**1.** Coat twelve 2½-inch muffin cups with cooking spray. Divide bread cubes among prepared cups. Remove ½ tsp. zest and squeeze juice from lemon.

**2.** In a medium bowl beat cream cheese with a mixer on medium until smooth. Gradually beat in ¼ cup honey and 3 Tbsp. of the lemon juice. Beat in egg and milk just until smooth; pour over bread cubes. Cover and chill overnight.

**3.** To serve, preheat oven to 350°F. Uncover and bake 20 to 25 minutes or until puffed and a knife comes out clean.

**4.** Meanwhile, in a blender or food processor combine 1 cup of the strawberries, 1 tsp. honey, lemon zest, and 1 tsp. of the lemon juice. Cover and blend or process until smooth. Stir in remaining 1 cup strawberries.

**5.** Cool toast cups in muffin cups 5 minutes. Remove cups from pan by running a thin metal spatula around the edges of the cups. Top with strawberry mixture and, if desired, additional lemon zest. Serve warm.

**PER SERVING** (2 cups each) **CAL** 211, **FAT** 6 g (2 g sat. fat), **CHOL** 14 mg, **SODIUM** 225 mg, **CARB** 34 g (3 g fiber, 20 g sugars), **PRO** 9 g

Overnight
Lemon-Cream
French Toast Cups

**Tip** To make dry bread cubes, preheat oven to 300°F. Cut 6 oz. (about 6 slices) fresh bread into ½-inch cubes. Spread cubes in a 15×10-inch baking pan. Bake 10 to 15 minutes or until dry, stirring twice; cool. (Cubes will continue to crisp as they cool.) Or let bread cubes stand, loosely covered, at room temperature 8 to 12 hours.

## Waffle Latkes

**28 g**
**CARB**

**SERVES** 4
**HANDS ON** 10 min.
**TOTAL** 30 min.

Nonstick cooking spray
- 8 cups frozen finely shredded hash brown potatoes
- ½ tsp. kosher salt
- ⅛ tsp. cracked black pepper
- ½ cup light sour cream
- 2 oz. thinly sliced smoked salmon (lox-style)
- 2 Tbsp. snipped fresh chives

**1.** Generously coat a waffle baker (do not use a Belgian-style baker) with cooking spray. Preheat waffle baker to high. Mound half of the hash browns evenly onto the waffle baker, putting about 1 cup hash browns on each of four squares of the baker; slowly press to close the lid. Cook about 10 minutes or until golden brown and crispy on the outside. Very carefully remove the entire waffle and set aside. Repeat with the remaining potatoes to make another waffle. Sprinkle waffles with the salt and pepper.

**2.** Cut each waffle into four squares. Arrange two waffle squares on each of four plates. Top with sour cream and salmon. Sprinkle with chives.

PER SERVING (*2 waffle squares each*)
**CAL** 168, **FAT** 4 g (2 g sat. fat), **CHOL** 15 mg, **SODIUM** 436 mg, **CARB** 28 g (3 g fiber, 0 g sugars), **PRO** 7 g

**Tip** To get the potatoes to stick together as much as possible, it is essential to use finely shredded hash brown potatoes for this recipe.

**Waffle Latkes**

# Individual Baked Oatmeal

**30 g**
**CARB**

| | |
|---|---|
| **SERVES** 12 | |
| **HANDS ON** 20 min. | |
| **TOTAL** 1 hr. 25 min. | |

- 2½ cups regular rolled oats
- ¼ cup oat bran
- ¼ cup steel-cut oats
- 2 tsp. baking powder
- ½ tsp. salt
- ½ tsp. ground cinnamon
- 2 cups milk
- 1 egg, lightly beaten
- ⅓ cup unsweetened applesauce
- ¼ cup granulated sugar*
- ¼ cup packed brown sugar*
- ¼ cup vegetable oil
- 2 cups fresh fruit, such as blueberries or blackberries, chopped pears or apples, and/or chopped strawberries
  Nonstick cooking spray
  Coarse sugar (optional)

**1.** In a large bowl stir together the first six ingredients (through cinnamon). In a medium bowl stir together the next six ingredients (through oil). Add milk mixture to oat mixture; stir until combined. Gently stir in fruit. Cover and chill 12 to 24 hours.

**2.** Preheat oven to 350°F. Coat twelve 6-oz. ramekins or custard cups or a 2-qt. square or rectangular baking dish with cooking spray. Divide oat mixture evenly among ramekins or spoon into baking dish. If desired, sprinkle with coarse sugar.

**3.** Bake 35 to 40 minutes for ramekins, 45 to 50 minutes for baking dish, or until tops are evenly brown and internal temperature reaches 160°F. Cool on a wire rack 15 minutes.

**PER SERVING** *(1 ramekin or ½ cup each)* **CAL** 198, **FAT** 7 g (1 g sat. fat), **CHOL** 19 mg, **SODIUM** 205 mg, **CARB** 30 g (3 g fiber, 14 g sugars), **PRO** 5 g

***Sugar Sub** Choose Splenda Sugar Blend and Splenda Brown Sugar Blend. Follow package directions to use ¼ cup equivalent for each.

**PER SERVING WITH SUB** Same as above, except **CAL** 184, **CARB** 26 g (10 g sugars)

Steel-Cut Oatmeal with
Chocolate-Bacon Topper

**QUICK TIP** Have oatmeal ready to eat when you are. Before going to bed, set a programmable slow cooker to turn on at a later time. If you don't have this kind of cooker, plug your cooker into a programmable outlet timer and set it as desired.

## Steel-Cut Oatmeal with Chocolate-Bacon Topper

**33 g**
**CARB**

**SERVES** 9
**HANDS ON** 10 min.
**SLOW COOK** 5 hr. 30 min.

- 6 cups water
- 2 cups steel-cut oats
- 1 tsp. salt
- ½ cup sugar-free maple-flavor syrup
- ¼ cup dried cranberries
- ¼ cup miniature semisweet chocolate pieces
- 4 slices bacon, crisp-cooked, crumbled, and cooled

**1.** In a 3½- or 4-qt. slow cooker combine the water, oats, and salt. Cover and cook on low 5½ to 6 hours or high 3 to 3½ hours.
**2.** For the topper, stir together syrup and dried cranberries; just before serving, stir in chocolate pieces. Top servings with topper and sprinkle with crumbled bacon.

PER SERVING (⅔ cooked oats + 1 Tbsp. topper each) **CAL** 202, **FAT** 6 g (2 g sat. fat), **CHOL** 4 mg, **SODIUM** 346 mg, **CARB** 33 g (4 g fiber, 7 g sugars), **PRO** 6 g

**To Make Ahead** Store leftover oatmeal in an airtight container up to 3 days in the refrigerator. To reheat one serving (⅔ cup), place oatmeal in a microwave-safe bowl. Add 1 to 2 Tbsp. water; stir to combine. Microwave on high 1½ to 2 minutes or until heated. Or place oatmeal in a small saucepan, stir in 1 to 2 Tbsp. water, and heat through on stove top.

## Apple-Cran-Oat Breakfast Cookies

**34 g**
CARB

**SERVES** 20
**HANDS ON** 25 min.
**TOTAL** 45 min.

- 2½ cups regular rolled oats
- 1 cup almond meal
- ½ cup whole wheat flour
- ¼ cup nonfat dry milk powder
- 1 tsp. baking soda
- 1 tsp. ground cinnamon
- ¼ tsp. salt
- 1 cup packed brown sugar*
- 2 eggs, lightly beaten
- 1 6-oz. carton plain fat-free Greek yogurt
- 2 tsp. orange zest
- 1½ tsp. vanilla
- 1½ cups chopped apple
- 1½ cups coarsely chopped fresh cranberries
- ⅔ cup powdered sugar*
- 1 Tbsp. orange juice

**1.** Preheat oven to 350°F. Line two cookie sheets with parchment paper.
**2.** In a large bowl combine the first seven ingredients (through salt). In a medium bowl combine the next four ingredients (through orange zest) and 1 tsp. of the vanilla; stir until well mixed. Stir egg mixture into oat mixture until evenly moistened. Fold in chopped apple and cranberries.
**3.** Using a ¼-cup measure, drop batter onto prepared cookie sheets. Flatten into circles about ½ inch thick. Bake about 15 minutes or until set. Cool 5 minutes on cookie sheets. Transfer to wire racks; cool completely.
**4.** For icing, in a small bowl whisk together powdered sugar, orange juice, and the remaining ½ tsp. vanilla. If necessary, stir in enough additional orange juice, ½ tsp. at a time, to make drizzling consistency. Drizzle icing over cookies.

**PER SERVING** (1 cookie each) **CAL** 201, **FAT** 5 g (1 g sat. fat), **CHOL** 19 mg, **SODIUM** 111 mg, **CARB** 34 g (4 g fiber, 17 g sugars), **PRO** 7 g

*Sugar Sub We do not recommend sugar subs for this recipe.

**To Store** Layer cookies between sheets of waxed paper in an airtight container; cover. Store in the refrigerator up to 3 days or freeze up to 3 months. Let stand at room temperature 30 minutes before serving.

**Apple-Cran-Oat Breakfast Cookies**

Cherry-Mocha Smoothie

## Cherry-Mocha Smoothie

**34 g**
**CARB**

**SERVES** 4
**TOTAL** 10 min.

- 2 cups frozen unsweetened pitted dark sweet cherries
- 2 cups unsweetened chocolate almond milk
- 2 5.3- to 6-oz. cartons vanilla fat-free Greek yogurt
- 1 medium banana
- ¼ cup unsweetened cocoa powder
- ¼ cup almond butter
- 2 tsp. instant espresso coffee powder
- 2 tsp. vanilla
- 4 cups ice cubes
  Dark chocolate shavings, chocolate-covered espresso beans (optional)

**1.** In a blender combine the first eight ingredients (through vanilla). Cover and blend until smooth. Add ice cubes; cover and blend until smooth. Pour into glasses. If desired, top with chocolate shavings, chocolate-covered espresso beans, and/or additional banana slices.

**PER SERVING** (2 cups each) **CAL** 272, **FAT** 12 g (2 g sat. fat), **CHOL** 2 mg, **SODIUM** 154 mg, **CARB** 34 g (7 g fiber, 21 g sugars), **PRO** 13 g

**Tip** If you prefer, place ice in tall glasses instead of blending ice with the smoothie. Pour smoothie over ice cubes.

**To Make Ahead** Pour smoothie into individual canning jars with tight-fitting lids. Store in the freezer. The night before serving, place jars in refrigerator to thaw. Stir before serving.

Quinoa-Pumpkin Seed Granola

## Quinoa-Pumpkin Seed Granola

**16 g**
**CARB**

**SERVES** 14
**HANDS ON** 20 min.
**TOTAL** 55 min.

- ¾ cup quinoa, rinsed and well drained
- ½ cup raw pumpkin seeds (pepitas)
- ½ cup whole and/or slivered almonds
- ¼ cup flaxseeds
- 2 Tbsp. honey
- 2 Tbsp. canola oil
- 1 tsp. ground cinnamon
- ½ tsp. coarse salt
- ½ cup dried cranberries or cherries, golden raisins, and/or snipped dried apricots

**1.** Preheat oven to 350°F. In a large bowl combine first four ingredients (through flaxseeds). In a small bowl microwave honey 20 seconds. Stir in oil, cinnamon, and salt. Pour over quinoa mixture; toss to coat. Spread in a 15×10-inch baking pan.

**2.** Bake about 18 minutes or until golden, stirring twice. Stir in dried fruit. Cool in pan on a wire rack 15 minutes.

**3.** Spread granola on a large sheet of foil; cool completely.

**PER SERVING** (¼ cup each) **CAL** 149, **FAT** 8 g (1 g sat. fat), **CHOL** 0 mg, **SODIUM** 42 mg, **CARB** 16 g (3 g fiber, 6 g sugars), **PRO** 5 g

**To Store** Place granola in an airtight container; cover. Store in the refrigerator up to 2 weeks.

# 2

# TASTY
# PARTY BITES

Expand your repertoire of go-to party recipes with these fresh and light appetizers. We've included a variety of flavorful options, from cold dips and spring rolls to hot baked finger foods to herby cheese crisps. You'll even find a cocktail and mocktail to show off your mixologist skills.

## Kale Dip

**1g**
**CARB**

**SERVES** 16
**HANDS ON** 20 min.
**TOTAL** 3 hr. 20 min.

1 6-oz. carton plain Greek yogurt
½ cup mayonnaise
1 cup finely chopped kale
½ cup chopped cucumber
1 Tbsp. snipped fresh dill
2 tsp. lemon juice
¼ tsp. salt
¼ tsp. black pepper
Fresh dill sprigs (optional)
Baked pita chips and/or cut-up
fresh vegetables

**1.** In a bowl stir together the first eight ingredients (through pepper). Cover and chill up to 3 hours. Stir before serving. If desired, top dip with fresh dill sprigs. Serve dip with chips and/or vegetables.

PER SERVING (2 Tbsp. dip each) **CAL** 60, **FAT** 6 g (1 g sat. fat), **CHOL** 4 mg, **SODIUM** 67 mg, **CARB** 1 g (0 g fiber, 1 g sugars), **PRO** 1 g

## Ricotta and Parmesan Dip

**1g**
**CARB**

**SERVES** 16
**HANDS ON** 15 min.
**TOTAL** 1 hr. 15 min.

- 1 15- to 16-oz. container whole milk ricotta cheese
- ¾ cup finely shredded Parmesan cheese (3 oz.)
- ¼ cup snipped fresh basil
- 2 Tbsp. snipped fresh oregano
- 2 Tbsp. snipped fresh chives
- 1 tsp. kosher salt or ½ tsp. regular salt
- 1 tsp. cracked black pepper
- 1 tsp. olive oil (optional) Baked pita chips and/or cut-up fresh vegetables

**1.** In a medium bowl beat ricotta with a mixer on medium 2 minutes. Add Parmesan. Beat until combined. Stir in the next five ingredients (through pepper). (If the dip seems a little dry, stir in olive oil.) Cover and chill 1 to 12 hours. Serve dip with pita chips and/or vegetables.

**PER SERVING** *(2 Tbsp. dip each)* **CAL** 63, **FAT** 4 g (3 g sat. fat), **CHOL** 16 mg, **SODIUM** 209 mg, **CARB** 1 g (0 g fiber, 0 g sugars), **PRO** 4 g

Ricotta and Parmesan Dip

## Asiago-Artichoke Dip

**6g**
**CARB**

**SERVES** 12
**HANDS ON** 20 min.
**TOTAL** 1 hr. 5 min.

- 1 14-oz. can artichoke hearts, rinsed and drained
- 1 cup arugula or fresh spinach, chopped
- 1 8-oz. carton light sour cream
- 3 Tbsp. all-purpose flour
- ½ cup reduced-fat mayonnaise
- ½ cup bottled roasted red sweet peppers, drained and finely chopped
- ½ cup finely shredded Asiago cheese or Parmesan cheese (2 oz.)
- ¼ cup thinly sliced green onions
  Cut-up fresh vegetables and/or baked pita chips or crackers

**1.** Preheat oven to 350°F. Place artichoke hearts in a fine-mesh sieve. To remove excess liquid, firmly press on artichoke hearts with paper towels. Chop artichoke hearts. Combine with arugula.

**2.** In a large bowl stir together sour cream and flour until combined. Stir in mayonnaise and roasted peppers. Stir in Asiago cheese, green onions, artichoke-arugula mixture. Transfer to an ungreased 9-inch pie plate.

**3.** Bake, uncovered, about 30 minutes or until edges are lightly browned and mixture is hot in center. If desired, sprinkle with 1 Tbsp. additional shredded Asiago. Cool 15 minutes before serving. Serve dip with vegetables and/or pita chips.

**PER SERVING** (¼ cup dip each) **CAL** 96, **FAT** 7 g (3 g sat. fat), **CHOL** 15 mg, **SODIUM** 192 mg, **CARB** 6 g (1 g fiber, 1 g sugars), **PRO** 2 g

Asiago-Artichoke Dip

## Spring Rolls with Cilantro Dipping Sauce

**16 g CARB** | **SERVES** 12
**TOTAL** 45 min.

- 2 oz. dried rice vermicelli noodles (rice sticks)
- 1 cup finely shredded napa cabbage
- ½ cup coarsely shredded carrot
- ½ cup snipped fresh cilantro
- 2 Tbsp. chopped dry-roasted cashews
- 2 tsp. reduced-sodium soy sauce
- 12 round rice papers
- 1½ cups shredded cooked chicken (about 8 oz.)
- ½ of a medium cucumber, seeded and cut into thin sticks
- 1 recipe Cilantro Dipping Sauce or Asian sweet chili sauce

**1.** In a 2-qt. saucepan cook noodles in boiling water 2 to 3 minutes or just until tender; drain. Rinse with cold water; drain again. Using kitchen scissors, snip noodles into small pieces.
**2.** For cabbage filling, in a large bowl combine cooked noodles and the next four ingredients (through cashews). Add soy sauce; toss to coat.
**3.** Fill a large bowl with warm water. Dip one rice paper into water a few seconds or just until moistened. Rice paper will still be firm but continue to soften. Place on work surface.
**4.** Arrange about 2 Tbsp. chicken across the lower third of the softened rice paper. Top with a layer of cucumber sticks. Top with ¼ cup cabbage filling. Fold bottom of rice paper over filling. Fold in sides; roll up tightly. Place, seam side down, on a serving plate. Repeat with the remaining rice papers, chicken, cucumber, and filling. Serve with Cilantro Dipping Sauce or Asian sweet chili sauce.

**Cilantro Dipping Sauce** In a blender combine ⅔ cup fresh cilantro leaves, ¼ cup lime juice, 2 Tbsp. water, 2 tsp. sugar,* 1 tsp. chopped fresh jalapeño

**QUICK TIP** Substitute shrimp, imitation crab meat (surimi), or tofu strips for the chicken.

Spring Rolls with Cilantro Dipping Sauce

pepper (tip, p. 156), 1 tsp. vegetable oil, and ⅛ tsp. salt. Cover and blend until nearly smooth.

**PER SERVING** *(1 spring roll each)* **CAL** 112, **FAT** 2 g (0 g sat. fat), **CHOL** 16 mg, **SODIUM** 81 mg, **CARB** 16 g (1 g fiber, 2 g sugars), **PRO** 6 g

***Sugar Sub** We do not recommend using a sugar sub for this recipe.

**To Make Ahead** Prepare spring rolls as directed. Layer spring rolls between damp paper towels in an airtight container; cover. Chill up to 4 hours.

## Tomato Tapenade Dip

**4g CARB**

**SERVES** 12
**HANDS ON** 15 min.
**TOTAL** 2 hr. 15 min.

- 1  14.5-oz. can diced tomatoes, drained
- ⅓  cup oil-packed dried tomato strips
- 2  Tbsp. balsamic vinegar
- 1  Tbsp. olive oil
- ⅛  tsp. cayenne pepper
- ⅓  cup chopped pitted Kalamata olives
- ⅓  cup chopped pitted green olives
- 2  cloves garlic, minced
   Pita chips, toasted baguette slices, and/or assorted crackers

**1.** In a bowl stir together the first five ingredients (through cayenne pepper). Stir in olives and garlic. Cover and chill 2 to 24 hours.

**2.** Serve dip with pita chips, baguette slices, and/or crackers.

**PER SERVING** *(2 Tbsp. dip each)* **CAL** 38, **FAT** 3 g (0 g sat. fat), **CHOL** 0 mg, **SODIUM** 202 mg, **CARB** 4 g (1 g fiber, 1 g sugars), **PRO** 1 g

**Tomato Tapenade Dip**

## Roasted Cherry Tomato Pizza Poppers

**8g CARB**

**SERVES** 14
**HANDS ON** 1 hr.
**TOTAL** 1 hr. 10 min.

- 2  pints red and/or yellow cherry or grape tomatoes, halved
- 1  Tbsp. olive oil
- 2  tsp. balsamic vinegar
- 2  to 4 cloves garlic, minced
- 1  tsp. snipped fresh oregano or ½ tsp. dried oregano, crushed
- 2  1-lb. portions frozen pizza dough, thawed
- ¼  cup olive oil
- 1  tsp. dried oregano, crushed
- 1  tsp. dried basil, crushed
- 12  to 14 oz. sliced mozzarella or provolone cheese, cut into 2-inch pieces

**1.** Preheat oven to 450°F. Place tomatoes in a 13×9-inch baking pan. Drizzle with the 1 Tbsp. oil and the vinegar. Sprinkle with garlic and 1 tsp. fresh or ½ tsp. dried oregano. Roast 10 to 12 minutes or until tomatoes are wilted, stirring occasionally.

**2.** Meanwhile, lightly grease a baking sheet. On a lightly floured surface roll one portion of pizza dough at a time into a 15×12-inch rectangle (if dough becomes difficult to roll, cover and let rest a few minutes). Cover and let rest 10 minutes. Using a 2- to 2½-inch round cutter, cut out dough; discard trimmings. Place dough rounds on prepared baking sheet. Prick all over with a fork.

**3.** In a small bowl combine the ¼ cup oil, 1 tsp. dried oregano, and dried basil; brush over dough rounds. Bake 7 minutes. Turn and top with cheese. Bake about 2 minutes more or until cheese is melted. Top with tomatoes and, if desired, *fresh basil*. Serve warm or at room temperature.

**PER SERVING** *(4 poppers each)* **CAL** 64, **FAT** 2 g (1 g sat. fat), **CHOL** 3 mg, **SODIUM** 104 mg, **CARB** 8 g (0 g fiber, 1 g sugars), **PRO** 2 g

**Roasted Cherry Tomato Pizza Poppers**

« **QUICK TIP** To make ahead, bake dough rounds, but do not top with cheese; cool. Place in an airtight container; cover. Store at room temperature up to 3 days. To serve, preheat oven to 350°F. Top rounds with cheese and bake about 2 minutes or until cheese is melted. Continue as directed.

## Parmesan Thyme Crisps

**1g**
**CARB**

**SERVES** 18
**HANDS ON** 25 min.
**TOTAL** 40 min.

1 cup freshly grated Parmesan
cheese
2 Tbsp. snipped fresh thyme

**1.** Preheat oven to 300°F. Line two or
three large baking sheets with
parchment paper. Using 2- to 3-inch
triangular or round cookie cutters as a
guide, draw 2- to 3-inch triangles or
circles 1 inch apart on the paper. Turn
paper over. (You should be able to see
markings through the paper.)
**2.** In a bowl stir together cheese and
thyme. Divide mixture among triangles
or circles, spreading to edges. Bake
12 to 14 minutes or until golden brown.
Cool on baking sheet until firm.
Transfer to a wire rack and let cool.

**PER SERVING** *(1 crisp each)* **CAL** 19,
**FAT** 1 g (1 g sat. fat), **CHOL** 4 mg,
**SODIUM** 80 mg, **CARB** 1 g (0 g fiber,
0 g sugars), **PRO** 1 g

《 **QUICK TIP** To make ahead, cover
and chill cheese and thyme mixture up
to 24 hours before baking.

## Picadillo Poppers

**7g**
**CARB**

**SERVES** servings
**HANDS ON** 45 min.
**TOTAL** 55 min.

- 8 oz. lean ground beef
- ⅓ cup chopped onion
- 1 8.8-oz. pouch cooked Spanish-style rice
- 1 cup shredded Monterey Jack cheese (4 oz.)
- ½ cup golden raisins
- ½ cup sliced pimiento-stuffed green olives
- 1 to 2 Tbsp. dry sherry or lime juice
- 24 fresh plump jalapeño peppers (tip, p. 156)
  Shredded Monterey Jack cheese (optional)

**1.** For filling, in a 10-inch skillet cook ground beef and onion over medium-high until meat is browned and onion is tender, stirring occasionally. Drain off fat. Stir in the next five ingredients (through sherry).

**2.** Cut a lengthwise slit in one side of each jalapeño pepper to create a pocket, being careful not to cut the pepper in half. Cut a very small crosswise slit on both ends of the long slit, making an L-shape opening. Leave stem intact and use a small spoon to remove seeds and scrape out membranes. Spoon filling into peppers.

**3.** Place filled peppers, slit sides up, in a greased grill basket or on a greased vegetable grilling pan. Grill peppers in basket, covered, over medium 8 to 12 minutes or until peppers are crisp-tender and filling is heated. If desired, sprinkle grilled peppers with additional cheese.

**To Broil** Preheat broiler. Prepare as directed through Step 2. Place filled peppers, slit sides up, on the unheated rack of a broiler pan. Broil 6 to 7 inches from the heat about 5 minutes or until peppers are crisp-tender and filling is heated. If desired, sprinkle with additional cheese.

Picadillo Poppers

**PER SERVING** *(1 popper each)* **CAL** 74, **FAT** 4 g (2 g sat. fat), **CHOL** 11 mg, **SODIUM** 107 mg, **CARB** 7 g (1 g fiber, 3 g sugars), **PRO** 4 g

Pea and Ricotta
Wontons

## Pea and Ricotta Wontons

**13 g**
**CARB**

| **SERVES** 6 |
|---|
| **HANDS ON** 25 min. |
| **TOTAL** 45 min. |

- ½ cup shelled fresh English peas
- 1 egg yolk
- 2 Tbsp. part-skim ricotta cheese
- 1 Tbsp. grated Parmesan cheese
- 12 wonton wrappers
  Nonstick cooking spray
- ½ cup dry white wine
- ¼ cup finely chopped shallots
- ⅛ tsp. salt
- ⅛ tsp. black pepper
- 3 Tbsp. cold butter, cut up
- 1 Tbsp. snipped fresh chives

**1.** Preheat oven to 375°F. Line two baking sheets with parchment paper or coat with cooking spray.

**2.** For filling, in a 1- or 1½-qt. saucepan cook peas in boiling water about 5 minutes or just until tender and bright green; drain. Immediately plunge into a bowl of ice water to cool; drain again and mash. Stir in egg yolk and both cheeses.

**3.** Spoon 1½ tsp. of the filling onto each wonton wrapper. Moisten two adjacent edges of wrapper with water and fold over filling to form a triangle; press lightly to seal. Place on the prepared baking sheets and coat tops with cooking spray. Bake about 10 minutes or until golden.

**4.** Meanwhile, for sauce, in a 6-inch skillet heat wine, shallots, salt, and pepper over medium until simmering. Cook about 3 minutes or until reduced by one-third. Reduce heat to low. Gradually whisk in butter, 1 Tbsp. at a time, adding another piece as the previous one melts. Stir in chives. Serve wontons with sauce.

**PER SERVING** (2 wontons + 1 Tbsp. sauce each) **CAL** 152, **FAT** 8 g (4 g sat. fat), **CHOL** 50 mg, **SODIUM** 209 mg, **CARB** 13 g (1 g fiber, 2 g sugars), **PRO** 4 g

## Mini Margherita Pizzas

**9g** CARB

**SERVES** servings
**TOTAL** 35 min.

- 1 14-oz. pkg. 12-inch thin-style Italian bread shell
- ½ cup roasted sweet pepper bruschetta topper, Kalamata olive bruschetta topper, or desired pizza sauce
- 6 oz. fresh mozzarella cheese, sliced
- 2 roma tomatoes, thinly sliced
  Freshly ground black pepper or crushed red pepper
  Small fresh basil leaves
  Grated Parmesan cheese (optional)

**1.** Preheat oven to 450°F. Line a large baking sheet with foil. Use a 2-inch round cutter to cut Italian bread shell into 18 to 20 circles (or use a knife to cut into 20 squares/pieces). Place bread pieces on prepared baking sheet.
**2.** Spread bruschetta topper on bread pieces. Top with mozzarella cheese and tomato slices. (If necessary, cut cheese and tomatoes to fit.)
**3.** Bake 8 to 10 minutes or until cheese is melted and bread pieces are crisp. Just before serving, sprinkle with pepper and top with basil leaves. If desired, sprinkle with Parmesan cheese.

**PER SERVING** *(1 mini pizza each)* **CAL** 83, **FAT** 4 g (1 g sat. fat), **CHOL** 8 mg, **SODIUM** 159 mg, **CARB** 9 g (0 g fiber, 0 g sugars), **PRO** 4 g

**To Make Ahead** Cut bread shell into circles or pieces. Place in an airtight container; cover. Store at room temperature up to 24 hours. Bake as directed.

**QUICK TIP** Mix things up a little by cutting the bread shell into both circles and squares.

Mini Margherita Pizzas

### Thai Deviled Eggs

**0g CARB**

**SERVES** 16
**HANDS ON** 25 min.
**TOTAL** 40 min.

8 eggs
⅓ cup mayonnaise
1 Tbsp. sriracha sauce
1 Tbsp. freshly squeezed lime juice
¼ tsp. salt
¼ tsp. ground ginger
  Pickled sliced ginger, fresh cilantro leaves, and/or chopped green onion (optional)

**1.** Place eggs in a single layer in a 4-qt. saucepan (do not stack eggs). Add enough cold water to cover the eggs by at least 1 inch. Bring to a rapid boil over high (water will have large, rapidly breaking bubbles). Remove from heat, cover, and let stand 12 minutes; drain. Run cold water over eggs or place them in ice water until cool enough to handle; drain and peel. Halve hard-boiled eggs and remove yolks. Set whites aside.

**2.** In a bowl stir together egg yolks and the next five ingredients (through ginger). Stuff egg white halves with yolk mixture, using 1 rounded tsp. of yolk mixture for each half and using the back of a second teaspoon to carefully push the yolk mixture off the first spoon into the cavity of the egg white. (To pipe the yolk mixture, place yolk mixture in a large resealable plastic bag, snip off one corner of the bag, and squeeze bag to pipe some of the yolk mixture into the cavity of each egg white half.) Cover and chill until serving time (up to 24 hours). If desired, top with pickled ginger, cilantro, and chopped green onions. Drizzle with additional sriracha sauce.

Thai Deviled Eggs

## California Sushi Rolls

**6 g CARB**

**SERVES** 16
**TOTAL** 30 min.

2  8-inch square sheets nori (seaweed)
1  recipe Sushi Rice Filling
   Desired fillings (such as small carrot, zucchini, or cucumber sticks; avocado slices; canned crabmeat; smoked salmon [lox-style]; and/or small cooked shrimp, peeled and deveined)
   Soy sauce and prepared wasabi paste and/or desired dipping sauce (optional)

**1.** Lay nori on a sushi mat lined with plastic wrap; with damp fingers, spread 1 cup of the Sushi Rice over each sheet to within 1 inch of one edge. Arrange desired vegetable or seafood fillings crosswise just off the center of the rice.
**2.** Roll seaweed toward the 1-inch unfilled edge. (For a tight, even roll, place your hands under the edge of the mat closest to you. While carefully lifting the edge of the nori, roll it away from you.) Press unfilled edge over top, brushing with water to seal if necessary.
**3.** Cut each roll into 8 pieces; arrange on a platter. If desired, serve with soy sauce, wasabi, and/or dipping sauce.

**Sushi Rice Filling** In a fine-mesh sieve wash **½ cup short grain rice** under cold running water, rubbing grains together with your fingers. In a 1-qt. saucepan combine rinsed rice and **¾ cup cold water**. Bring to boiling; reduce heat. Simmer, covered, 15 minutes (rice should be sticky). Remove from heat. In a small bowl stir together **2 tsp. rice vinegar, 1 tsp. sugar,** and **½ tsp. salt**. Stir vinegar mixture into rice in saucepan; cover and cool about 45 minutes or until room temperature. (Rice can be covered and chilled up to 3 days.)

**PER SERVING** *(1 piece each)* **CAL** 28, **FAT** 0 g, **CHOL** 1 mg, **SODIUM** 77 mg, **CARB** 6 g (0 g fiber, 0 g sugars), **PRO** 1 g

**PER SERVING** *(1 deviled egg half each)* **CAL** 68, **FAT** 6 g (1 g sat. fat), **CHOL** 95 mg, **SODIUM** 120 mg, **CARB** 0 g (0 g fiber, 0 g sugars), **PRO** 3 g

**Tip** For easier peeling, store eggs in the refrigerator about 1 week before cooking.

California Sushi Rolls

## Stuffed Mini Sweet Peppers

**3 g CARB**

**SERVES** 15
**TOTAL** 45 min.

- 15 to 20 miniature sweet peppers
- 1 medium avocado, halved, seeded, peeled, and cut up
- 4 oz. cream cheese, softened
- ¼ cup basil pesto
- 2 tsp. lemon juice
  Thinly sliced fresh basil (optional)

**1.** Cut miniature sweet peppers in half lengthwise. Remove seeds and membranes.
**2.** For filling, in a food processor combine the next four ingredients (through lemon juice). Cover and process until smooth. Spoon filling into pepper halves.
**3.** Serve immediately or cover loosely and chill up to 4 hours. If desired, top with thinly sliced basil before serving.

**PER SERVING** (2 stuffed pepper halves each)
**CAL** 69, **FAT** 6 g (2 g sat. fat), **CHOL** 10 mg, **SODIUM** 66 mg, **CARB** 3 g (1 g fiber, 2 g sugars), **PRO** 1 g

**Orange Pear-tini**

## Orange Pear-tini

**18 g**
CARB

**SERVES** 1
**HANDS ON** 20 min.
**TOTAL** 40 min.

- ¼ cup Pear Puree
- 3 Tbsp. (1½ oz.) vodka
- 1 Tbsp. (½ oz.) orange liqueur
  Ice cubes
- 3 Tbsp. (1½ oz.) club soda
  Cinnamon stick (optional)
  Orange twist and/or pear slice
  (optional)

**1.** In a cocktail shaker combine Pear Puree, vodka, and orange liqueur. Add ice cubes; cover and shake 10 to 15 seconds. Strain liquid into a martini glass. Add club soda. If desired, serve with cinnamon stick and orange twist and/or pear slice.

**Pear Puree** Peel **2 medium pears** and cut into ½-inch pieces (about 2 cups). In a 2-qt. saucepan bring pears, **1¼ cups water**, and **¼ cup each sugar\*** and **orange juice** to boiling, stirring to dissolve sugar. Reduce heat. Simmer, covered, about 20 minutes or until pears are soft. Cool slightly. Transfer mixture to a blender or food processor. Cover and blend or process 30 seconds or until smooth. Strain through a fine-mesh sieve into a bowl; discard solids. Makes 2⅓ cups.

**PER SERVING** (6 oz.) **CAL** 190, **FAT** 0 g, **CHOL** 0 mg, **SODIUM** 11 mg, **CARB** 18 g (1 g fiber, 11 g sugars), **PRO** 0 g

**\*Sugar Sub** We do not recommend a sugar sub for this recipe.

## Honeydew-Basil Nojitos

**14 g**
CARB

**SERVES** 8
**TOTAL** 25 min.

- ½ cup large fresh basil leaves, torn
- ½ cup lime juice
- 2 tsp. sugar\*
- 2 3-lb. honeydew melons, peeled, seeded, and cubed
  Ice cubes
  Carbonated water (optional)
  Honeydew melon spears or balls (optional)

**1.** In a large pitcher combine basil leaves, lime juice, and sugar. Using a muddler or the back of a wooden spoon, mash ingredients together well, making sure most of the sugar is dissolved.
**2.** Place about one-fourth of the melon cubes in a food processor or blender. Cover and process or blend until smooth. Press puree through a fine-mesh sieve; discard solids. Repeat with the remaining melon cubes, one-fourth at a time. Measure out 4 cups melon juice and add to the pitcher.

**3.** Fill eight glasses with ice. Pour juice mixture into ice-filled glasses. If desired, add a splash of carbonated water to each glass. If desired, add melon spears or balls to each glass. Serve immediately.

**PER SERVING** (1 drink each) **CAL** 54, **FAT** 0 g, **CHOL** 0 mg, **SODIUM** 23 mg, **CARB** 14 g (1 g fiber, 12 g sugars), **PRO** 1 g

**\*Sugar Sub** Choose Splenda Granular. Follow package directions to use 2 tsp. equivalent.

**PER SERVING WITH SUB** Same as above, except **CAL** 50, **CARB** 13 g

**Honeydew-Basil Nojitos**

# 3

# COMFORTING
# SOUPS & STEWS

The days around the holidays can get busier than you expect. A steaming bowl of soup is the perfect fix when you want a simple, complete meal. Several of these recipes use a slow cooker. You can prep them in the morning and forget them until mealtime. And these soups are great when everyone is on a different schedule.

## Mushroom and Beef Ravioli Soup

**28 g**
**CARB**

**SERVES** 6
**TOTAL** 20 min.

1  Tbsp. olive oil
1  small onion, halved and thinly sliced
2  cups sliced cremini mushrooms (6 oz.)
2  miniature red sweet peppers, stemmed and sliced (about ½ cup)
1  32-oz. box unsalted beef broth or mushroom broth
1  20-oz. pkg. frozen beef ravioli
   Fresh thyme leaves
   Black pepper

**1.** In a 4-qt. pot heat olive oil over medium-high. Add onion, mushrooms, and sweet peppers; cook and stir about 4 minutes or until tender. Stir in broth; bring to boiling. Stir in ravioli; return to boiling. Reduce heat. Cook, uncovered, 5 to 8 minutes or until pasta is tender, stirring occasionally. Sprinkle with thyme and black pepper before serving.

**PER SERVING** *(1 cup each)* **CAL** 225, **FAT** 7 g (2 g sat. fat), **CHOL** 30 mg, **SODIUM** 473 mg, **CARB** 28 g (2 g fiber, 2 g sugars), **PRO** 12 g

## Beef Goulash Soup

**16 g**
**CARB**

**SERVES** 4
**HANDS ON** 30 min.
**TOTAL** 50 min.

- 6 oz. boneless beef top sirloin steak
- 1 tsp. olive oil
- ½ cup chopped onion
- 2 cups water
- 1 14.5-oz. can beef broth
- 1 14.5-oz. can no-salt-added diced tomatoes, undrained
- ½ cup thinly sliced carrot
- 1 tsp. unsweetened cocoa powder
- 1 clove garlic, minced
- 1 cup thinly sliced cabbage
- ½ cup dried wide noodles (1 oz.)
- 2 tsp. paprika
- ¼ cup light sour cream
  Snipped fresh parsley (optional)

**1.** Trim fat from meat. Cut meat into ½-inch cubes. In a 3-qt. saucepan cook and stir meat in hot oil over medium-high about 6 minutes or until browned. Add onion; cook and stir 3 minutes more or until onion softens.

**2.** Stir in the next six ingredients (through garlic). Bring to boiling; reduce heat. Simmer, uncovered, about 15 minutes or until meat is tender.

**3.** Stir in the cabbage, noodles, and paprika. Simmer, uncovered, 5 to 7 minutes more or until noodles are tender but still firm. Remove from heat. Top each serving with some of the sour cream. If desired, sprinkle with parsley and additional paprika.

**PER SERVING** (1½ cups each) **CAL** 188, **FAT** 7 g (3 g sat. fat), **CHOL** 36 mg, **SODIUM** 397 mg, **CARB** 16 g (3 g fiber, 6 g sugars), **PRO** 14 g

**Beef Goulash Soup**

**Chipotle BBQ Beef
Meatball Chili**

## Chipotle BBQ Beef Meatball Chili

**36 g**
CARB

**SERVES** 8
**HANDS ON** 30 min.
**SLOW COOK** 6 hr.

- 2 14.5-oz. cans no-salt-added fire-roasted diced tomatoes
- 1 15-oz. can hominy, rinsed and drained
- 1 15-oz. can no-salt-added red beans or kidney beans, rinsed and drained
- 1½ cups water
- 1 6-oz. can no-salt-added tomato paste
- 1 cup frozen sweet corn kernels
- ½ cup chopped red or green sweet pepper
- ½ cup finely chopped red onion
- ¼ cup barbecue sauce
- 1 Tbsp. chili powder
- ½ tsp. salt
- 1 recipe BBQ Meatballs

**1.** In a 4- to 6-qt. slow cooker combine the first 11 ingredients (through salt). Stir until well combined. Add partially cooked BBQ Meatballs. Stir gently.
**2.** Cover and cook on low 6 to 7 hours or on high 3 to 3½ hours. If desired, top with *fresh cilantro*.

**BBQ Meatballs** Preheat broiler. Line a 15×10-inch baking pan with foil. In a large bowl lightly beat **1 egg**. Whisk in **1 Tbsp. barbecue sauce, 1½ tsp. coarse-ground mustard**, and **¼ tsp. ground chipotle pepper**. Stir in **½ cup finely chopped red onion** and **⅓ cup cornmeal**. Add **1½ lb. 90%-lean ground beef**; mix well. Shape meat mixture into 1-inch balls. Place meatballs 1 inch apart in prepared pan. Broil meatballs (in batches if necessary) 6 inches from heat 7 minutes or until lightly browned (meatballs will not be cooked through).

**PER SERVING** *(1½ cups each)* **CAL** 327, **FAT** 9 g (3 g sat. fat), **CHOL** 78 mg, **SODIUM** 503 mg, **CARB** 36 g (8 g fiber, 11 g sugars), **PRO** 24 g

Creamy Ham and Potato Chowder

## Creamy Ham and Potato Chowder

**27 g**
CARB

**SERVES** 6
**HANDS ON** 20 min.
**SLOW COOK** 3 hr. 30 min.

- 12 oz. tiny yellow potatoes, cut into ¾-inch pieces
- 1 cup chopped onion
- 2 14.5-oz. cans reduced-sodium chicken broth
- ¼ cup cornstarch
- ½ tsp. dried thyme, crushed
- ¼ tsp. black pepper
- 1 12-oz. can evaporated fat-free milk (1½ cups)
- ½ cup diced cooked lean ham
- 1 cup coarsely shredded carrots
- 1 cup broccoli florets, steamed
- ¼ cup shredded cheddar cheese (1 oz.)
- 2 tsp. snipped fresh thyme

**1.** In a 4-qt. slow cooker combine potatoes and onion. Add broth. Cover and cook on high 3 hours.
**2.** In a medium bowl combine cornstarch, dried thyme, and pepper. Whisk in evaporated milk. Slowly stir the cornstarch mixture, ham, and carrots into the hot soup. Cover and cook 30 minutes more, stirring the soup occasionally.
**3.** Serve soup topped with broccoli, cheese, and fresh thyme.

**PER SERVING** *(1⅓ cups each)* **CAL** 171, **FAT** 2 g (1 g sat. fat), **CHOL** 12 mg, **SODIUM** 566 mg, **CARB** 27 g (3 g fiber, 10 g sugars), **PRO** 11 g

**Pork, Farro, Bean,
and Sweet Potato Stew**

## Pork, Farro, Bean, and Sweet Potato Stew

**48 g CARB**

**SERVES** 6
**HANDS ON** 20 min.
**SLOW COOK** 2 hr. 30 min.

3 cups reduced-sodium chicken
or vegetable broth
1 14.5-oz. can no-salt-added
fire-roasted diced tomatoes,
undrained
1⅔ cups bite-size pieces peeled
sweet potato
1 cup whole farro
1 cup chopped leeks
1 cup coarsely chopped celery
4 cloves garlic, minced
½ tsp. salt
½ tsp. crushed red pepper
4 cups coarsely chopped fresh
collard greens, green cabbage,
green kale, or Swiss chard
1 15-oz. can no-salt-added pinto
beans, rinsed and drained
8 oz. shredded cooked pork
shoulder
3 Tbsp. lemon juice
⅓ cup snipped fresh basil

**1.** In a 3½- or 4-qt. slow cooker
combine the first nine ingredients
(through crushed red pepper). Cover
and cook on high 2 hours or until farro
is tender but still chewy.
**2.** Stir in greens, beans, and meat.
Cover and cook 30 to 60 minutes more
or until greens are tender. Stir in lemon
juice. Sprinkle servings with basil.

**PER SERVING** *(1½ cups each)* **CAL** 351,
**FAT** 8 g (3 g sat. fat), **CHOL** 37 mg,
**SODIUM** 555 mg, **CARB** 48 g (10 g fiber,
5 g sugars), **PRO** 21 g

**White Chicken Chili**

**Creamy Corn Soup with Crispy Bacon**

## White Chicken Chili

**32 g**
**CARB**

**SERVES** 8
**HANDS ON** 20 min.
**SLOW COOK** 4 hr.

- 3 15-oz. cans no-salt-added great Northern beans, rinsed and drained
- 4 cups reduced-sodium chicken broth
- 1 lb. skinless, boneless chicken breast halves
- 2 cups finely chopped onions
- 1½ cups chopped desired-color sweet peppers
- 2 4-oz. cans diced green chile peppers, undrained
- 4 cloves garlic, minced
- 2 tsp. ground cumin
- 1 tsp. dried oregano, crushed
- ½ tsp. salt
- ¼ tsp. cayenne pepper
- 1½ cups shredded Monterey Jack cheese (6 oz.) (optional)
  Plain fat-free Greek yogurt (optional)
  Fresh cilantro leaves (optional)

**1.** In a 4- to 5-qt. slow cooker combine the first 11 ingredients (through cayenne pepper). Cover and cook on low 4 to 5 hours or high 2 to 3 hours.
**2.** Remove chicken; shred using two forks. Return shredded chicken to cooker. If desired, top servings with cheese, yogurt, and/or cilantro.

**PER SERVING** (1½ cups each ) **CAL** 239, **FAT** 3 g (0 g sat. fat), **CHOL** 41 mg, **SODIUM** 582 mg, **CARB** 32 g (10 g fiber, 5 g sugars), **PRO** 22 g

## Creamy Corn Soup with Crispy Bacon

**31 g**
**CARB**

**SERVES** 4
**HANDS ON** 55 min.
**TOTAL** 1 hr. 5 min.

- 2 Tbsp. unsalted butter
- 1 cup chopped onion
- 1 cup thinly sliced celery
- ½ cup thinly sliced carrot
- 2 cloves garlic, minced
- ¼ tsp. salt
- 1 Tbsp. all-purpose flour
- 2 cups fat-free milk
- 1 14.5-oz. can reduced-sodium chicken broth
- 2 cups frozen whole kernel corn, thawed
- 2 sprigs fresh thyme or ½ tsp. dried thyme, crushed
- 2 bay leaves
- 4 slices lower-sodium, less-fat bacon, crisp-cooked and crumbled
  Cracked black pepper (optional)

**1.** In a 4-qt. Dutch oven melt butter over medium. Add the next five ingredients (through salt); cook about 10 minutes or until vegetables are softened, stirring occasionally. If desired, remove about ½ cup of the vegetables to use as a topper. Stir flour into the remaining vegetables. Cook and stir 1 minute more.
**2.** Gradually whisk in milk and broth. Stir in corn, thyme, and bay leaves. Bring to boiling; reduce heat. Simmer, covered, 10 minutes, stirring frequently. Remove from heat; cool 10 minutes.
**3.** Remove and discard thyme sprigs and bay leaves. Using an immersion blender, blend soup until smooth. (Or working in batches, transfer soup to a blender; cover and blend until smooth. Return all of the soup to Dutch oven.) Heat through. Top servings with the reserved vegetables, crumbled bacon, and, if desired, pepper.

**PER SERVING** (1⅓ cups each) **CAL** 231, **FAT** 8 g (4 g sat. fat), **CHOL** 21 mg, **SODIUM** 540 mg, **CARB** 31 g (3 g fiber, 11 g sugars), **PRO** 11 g

Chicken Lentil-Farro Bowl

**QUICK TIP**
Be sure to use pearled farro for this recipe. It cooks faster than whole farro because its hull has been removed.

## Chicken Lentil-Farro Bowl

**35 g**
**CARB**

**SERVES** 6
**HANDS ON** 25 min.
**TOTAL** 55 min.

- 7 to 8 cups chicken broth
- ⅔ cup pearled farro
- ½ cup dried French lentils
- 1 Tbsp. olive oil
- 1½ cups coarsely chopped fennel bulb
- 3 carrots, halved lengthwise and cut up
- 2 small leeks, trimmed and sliced
- 3 Tbsp. snipped fresh parsley
- 3 Tbsp. snipped fresh fennel fronds (optional)
- 2 cloves garlic, minced
- 2 cups shredded cooked chicken
- ½ tsp. salt
- ½ tsp. black pepper
  Lemon slices (optional)

**1.** In a 4-qt. Dutch oven bring broth to boiling. Add farro and lentils. Return to boiling; reduce heat. Simmer, uncovered, 25 to 30 minutes or until tender.

**2.** Meanwhile, in a 10-inch skillet heat oil over medium. Add fennel, carrots, and leeks; cook about 5 minutes or until tender, stirring occasionally. In a bowl stir together parsley, fennel fronds (if using), and garlic.

**3.** Stir sautéed vegetables, chicken, salt, and pepper into broth mixture. Cook and stir until heated. If desired, float a lemon slice on each serving; top with parsley mixture.

**PER SERVING** (1⅓ cups each) **CAL** 312, **FAT** 7 g (2 g sat. fat), **CHOL** 61 mg, **SODIUM** 613 mg, **CARB** 35 g (6 g fiber, 4 sugars), **PRO** 28 mg

## Herbed Chicken Meatball Stew

**24 g** CARB

| | |
|---|---|
| **SERVES** | 8 |
| **HANDS ON** | 30 min. |
| **TOTAL** | 1 hr. 5 min. |

|   |   |
|---|---|
| 2 | Tbsp. butter |
| 1½ | cups finely chopped onions |
| 4 | cloves garlic, minced |
| 4 | cups reduced-sodium chicken broth |
| 3 | Tbsp. lemon juice |
| 3 | tsp. herbes de Provence |
| 12 | oz. baby golden potatoes, halved or quartered |
| 1 | egg, lightly beaten |
| ¼ | cup fine dry bread crumbs |
| ¼ | tsp. salt |
| 1½ | lb. uncooked ground chicken |
| 3 | oz. soft goat cheese (chèvre) |
| 1 | 15- to 16-oz. can no-salt-added Great Northern beans, rinsed and drained |
| 12 | oz. fresh green beans, trimmed and cut up |
| ¼ | cup chopped green olives |

**1.** In a 4-qt. Dutch oven melt butter over medium. Add onions and garlic; cook about 5 minutes or until onion softens, stirring occasionally. Remove half of the mixture to a large bowl. Add broth, lemon juice, and 2 tsp. of the herbes de Provence to pot; bring to boiling. Add potatoes; reduce heat. Simmer, covered, 15 minutes.

**2.** Meanwhile, add egg, bread crumbs, the remaining 1 tsp. herbes de Provence, and salt to the cooled onion mixture. Add chicken and goat cheese; mix well. Shape into 1½-inch balls. Add meatballs, Great Northern beans, and green beans to pot. Return to boiling; reduce heat. Simmer, covered, about 15 minutes more or until meatballs are done (165°F) and vegetables are tender. Top servings with olives.

**To Slow Cook** Prepare as directed, except do not cook onion and garlic in butter. In a 4- to 6-qt. slow cooker combine 1 cup of the onions, two cloves of the garlic, the broth, lemon juice, 2 tsp. of the herbes de Provence, and potatoes. In a bowl combine the egg, the remaining ½ cup onion, remaining garlic, bread crumbs, remaining 1 tsp. herbes de Provence, the goat cheese, salt, and chicken; mix well. Shape into 1½-inch balls; add to cooker. Cover and cook on low 8 hours or high 4 hours. Stir in Great Northern beans and green beans. Cover and cook on high 30 minutes more. Top servings with olives.

**PER SERVING** (about 1⅓ cups each)
**CAL** 321, **FAT** 15 g (6 g sat. fat), **CHOL** 112 mg, **SODIUM** 603 mg, **CARB** 24 g (6 g fiber, 4 g sugars), **PRO** 24 g

Herbed Chicken Meatball Stew

Spicy Chicken-Coconut
Noodle Soup

## Spicy Chicken-Coconut Noodle Soup

**16 g**
**CARB**

**SERVES** 6
**HANDS ON** 20 min.
**TOTAL** 40 min.

- 1 red sweet pepper, cut into thin bite-size strips (1 cup)
- 1 cup stemmed shiitake mushrooms or button mushrooms, thinly sliced
- 1 medium shallot, thinly sliced
- 4 tsp. toasted sesame oil
- 2 6- to 8-oz. skinless, boneless chicken breast halves
- 6 cups unsalted chicken broth or stock
- ½ cup thinly sliced celery
- 3 Tbsp. reduced-sodium soy sauce
- ½ tsp. crushed red pepper
- 2 cups dried wide egg noodles
- 2 medium carrots, thinly sliced
- 1 cup canned unsweetened light coconut milk
- ½ cup chopped fresh cilantro
- ¼ cup unsweetened large flaked coconut, toasted (optional)

**1.** In a 4-qt. saucepan cook sweet pepper, mushrooms, and shallot in 2 tsp. of the oil over medium 5 to 7 minutes or until vegetables are tender, stirring occasionally. Remove vegetables from saucepan.
**2.** Add the remaining 2 tsp. oil to the saucepan. Add chicken. Cook over medium 6 to 8 minutes or until browned, turning once. Add the next four ingredients (through crushed red pepper). Bring to boiling; reduce heat. Simmer, covered, 5 minutes. Stir in noodles and carrots. Return to boiling; reduce heat. Simmer, covered, 5 to 7 minutes or until chicken is no longer pink, stirring occasionally.
**3.** Transfer chicken to a cutting board. Cut chicken into cubes. Return chicken to soup. Stir in mushroom mixture and coconut milk. Cook and stir over medium 1 to 2 minutes or just until heated. Stir in half of the cilantro.
**4.** Sprinkle individual servings with remaining cilantro and, if desired, toasted coconut. If desired, serve with *sriracha sauce.*

**PER SERVING** *(1½ cups each)* **CAL** 221, **FAT** 8 g (3 g sat. fat), **CHOL** 52 mg, **SODIUM** 433 mg, **CARB** 16 g (2 g fiber, 4 g sugars), **PRO** 20 g

## Chicken Pho

**27 g**
**CARB**

**SERVES** 6
**HANDS ON** 25 min.
**SLOW COOK** 7 hr. 10 min.

- 6 oz. fresh shiitake mushrooms
- 1 3-inch piece fresh ginger, peeled and sliced
- 1 Tbsp. coriander seeds
- 4 whole cloves
- 2 lb. bone-in chicken thighs, skin removed
- 4 cups water
- 1 32-oz. carton unsalted chicken stock
- 1 large onion, sliced
- 1 oz. dried porcini mushrooms, rinsed, drained, and broken
- 1 Tbsp. packed brown sugar*
- 5 cloves garlic, sliced
- 1 tsp. salt
- 4 oz. dried rice noodles, soaked Julienned carrots, slivered red onion, thinly sliced fresh jalapeño chile peppers (tip, *p. 156*), fresh cilantro, Thai basil, mint leaves, sriracha sauce, and/or lime wedges (optional)

**1.** Remove and reserve stems from shiitake mushrooms. Thinly slice caps and chill until needed. Place shiitake stems, ginger, coriander seeds, and cloves on a double-thick 8-inch square of 100%-cotton cheesecloth. Bring up corners; tie closed with 100%-cotton string.
**2.** In a 5- to 6-qt. slow cooker combine spice bag and the next eight ingredients (through salt). Cover and cook on low 7 to 8 hours or high 3½ to 4 hours. Remove and discard spice bag.
**3.** Remove chicken from cooker. Remove meat from bones; discard bones. Coarsely shred chicken using two forks; cover and keep warm. Stir the reserved shiitake caps and noodles into broth mixture. Cover and cook 10 minutes more.
**4.** Ladle noodle mixture into shallow bowls. Add shredded chicken and desired toppers.

Chicken Pho

**PER SERVING** *(1¾ cups each)* **CAL** 246, **FAT** 4 g (1 g sat. fat), **CHOL** 85 mg, **SODIUM** 623 mg, **CARB** 27 g (3 g fiber, 7 g sugars), **PRO** 24 g

**PER SERVING WITH SUB** Same as original, except **CAL** 243, **CARB** 26 g (5 g sugars)

**\*Sugar Sub** Choose Splenda Brown Sugar Blend. Follow package directions to use 1 Tbsp. equivalent.

**Tip** To soak rice noodles, in a large bowl combine noodles and enough boiling water to cover. Let stand 3 to 7 minutes or until noodles are tender but still firm, stirring occasionally.

## Spring Lamb and Fava Bean Soup

**19 g**
**CARB**

SERVES 8
HANDS ON 20 min.
SLOW COOK 8 hr. 15 min.

- 1 lb. boneless lamb shoulder or beef chuck, trimmed of fat and cut into 1-inch pieces
- 1 Tbsp. olive oil
- 4 cups 50%-less-sodium beef broth
- 1½ cups water
- 8 oz. morel, oyster, or cremini mushrooms, sliced
- 1 8.8-oz. pkg. peeled and steamed fava beans, rinsed and drained, or 1½ cups frozen fava beans, thawed
- 1 cup sliced carrots
- 2 medium leeks, sliced
- ⅓ cup regular pearled barley
- 1 tsp. snipped fresh thyme
- 1 tsp. snipped fresh rosemary
- 1 cup fresh English peas, shelled, or frozen peas, thawed
- ¼ tsp. salt
- ¼ tsp. black pepper
- 1 recipe Lemon Gremolata

1. In a 10-inch skillet cook lamb in hot oil over medium until browned; drain off fat.
2. In a 4- to 5-qt. slow cooker combine lamb and the next nine ingredients (through rosemary).
3. Cover and cook on low 8 to 10 hours or high 4 to 5 hours. Stir in peas. Cover and cook 15 minutes more. Season to taste with salt and pepper. Top servings with Lemon Gremolata.

**Lemon Gremolata** In a small bowl combine ¼ cup snipped fresh Italian parsley, 1 Tbsp. lemon zest, and 2 cloves garlic, minced.

PER SERVING (1¼ cups each) CAL 202, FAT 7 g (2 g sat. fat), CHOL 36 mg, SODIUM 359 mg, CARB 19 g (6 g fiber, 4 g sugars), PRO 17 g

Spring Lamb and
Fava Bean Soup

## Clam Chowder

**27 g**
**CARB**

**SERVES** 6
**HANDS ON** 35 min.
**SLOW COOK** 7 hr. 30 min.

- 1½ cups chopped celery
- 1½ cups chopped onions
- 1½ cups chopped red-skin potatoes
- 1¼ cups water
- 1 cup chopped carrots
- 1 cup reduced-sodium chicken broth or low-sodium vegetable broth
- 1 8-oz. bottle clam juice
- 1½ tsp. dried thyme, crushed
- ½ tsp. coarse-ground black pepper
- 1 12-oz. can evaporated fat-free milk
- 3 Tbsp. cornstarch
- 2 6.5-oz. cans chopped clams, drained
- 2 Tbsp. dry sherry (optional)
- 1 tsp. red wine vinegar
- 2 slices turkey bacon, cooked and chopped
  Chopped green onions (optional)

**1.** In a 3½- or 4-qt. slow cooker combine the first nine ingredients (through pepper). Cover and cook on low 7 hours or high 3½ hours.

**2.** If using low, turn to high. In a medium bowl whisk evaporated milk into cornstarch. Stir milk mixture, clams, and, if desired, sherry into vegetable mixture. Cover and cook 30 to 60 minutes more or until bubbly around edges.

**3.** Before serving, stir in vinegar. Sprinkle servings with bacon and, if desired, green onions.

**PER SERVING** *(1⅓ cups each)* **CAL** 222, **FAT** 2 g (1 g sat. fat), **CHOL** 48 mg, **SODIUM** 599 mg, **CARB** 27 g (3 g fiber, 10 g sugars), **PRO** 25 g

Clam Chowder

**QUICK TIP** For easy cleanup, line your slow cooker with a disposable slow cooker liner. Add ingredients as directed in recipe. Spoon chowder out of cooker and dispose of the liner. Do not lift or transport the disposable liner with food inside.

**QUICK TIP** French lentils are small, round, and dark. They cook faster and hold their shape better than their brown and yellow cousins, which shouldn't be used as substitutes. Look for them in the health food and bulk food sections of your supermarket.

French Lentil and Salmon Soup

# French Lentil and Salmon Soup

**35 g**
CARB

**SERVES** 6
**HANDS ON** 20 min.
**TOTAL** 50 min.

- 12 oz. fresh or frozen skinless salmon
- 1 medium fennel bulb
- 6 cups unsalted vegetable broth or stock
- 4 medium carrots, cut into 1-inch pieces
- 1 cup dried French lentils
- 4 cloves garlic, minced
- 1 bay leaf
- ¼ tsp. salt
- ¼ tsp. black pepper
- 2 Tbsp. snipped fresh dill or 1½ tsp. dried dill
- 3 cups spinach
- 3 Tbsp. lemon juice

**1.** Thaw fish if frozen. Coarsely snip 2 Tbsp. of the fennel fronds. Set aside for garnish. Cut off and discard upper stalks of fennel bulb. Remove any wilted outer layers; cut off and discard a thin slice from base of fennel. Halve, core, and chop remaining fennel.
**2.** In a 4-qt. saucepan combine chopped fennel and the next seven ingredients (through pepper). Bring to boiling; reduce heat. Simmer, covered, about 25 minutes or until lentils are just tender, stirring occasionally.
**3.** Meanwhile, pat salmon dry with paper towels. Cut into 1-inch pieces. Add salmon and dried dill (if using) to soup when lentils are tender. Return to boiling; reduce heat. Simmer, uncovered, 4 to 5 minutes or just until fish flakes. Remove from heat. Remove and discard bay leaf.
**4.** Add fresh dill (if using), spinach, and lemon juice to soup. Top with reserved fennel fronds and additional pepper.

**PER SERVING** (1⅔ cups each) **CAL** 254, **FAT** 4 g (1 g sat. fat), **CHOL** 31 mg, **SODIUM** 387 mg, **CARB** 35 g (6 g fiber, 8 g sugars), **PRO** 20 g

# Cajun Red Beans and Rice Soup

**35 g**
CARB

**SERVES** 6
**HANDS ON** 20 min.
**TOTAL** 50 min.

- 1 Tbsp. canola oil
- ½ of a 12-oz. pkg. fully cooked smoked andouille chicken sausage or sun-dried tomato chicken sausage links, thinly sliced, such as Al Fresco
- 1 Tbsp. minced garlic
- ½ tsp. salt
- ½ tsp. lite or salt-free creole or Cajun seasoning
- ½ tsp. dried thyme, crushed
- ½ tsp. smoked paprika or 1 tsp. regular paprika
- 1 32-oz. carton unsalted chicken stock
- 1 cup water
- ½ cup uncooked long grain brown rice
- 1 14-oz. pkg. frozen onion and pepper stir-fry blend vegetables
- 2 cups stemmed and coarsely chopped fresh collard greens or fresh baby spinach
- 1 15-oz. can reduced-sodium red kidney beans or no-salt-added pinto beans, rinsed and drained
- 1 14.5-oz. can no-salt-added diced tomatoes with basil, oregano, and garlic

**1.** In a 5- to 6-qt. pot heat oil over medium. Add sausage; cook 4 minutes, stirring occasionally. Transfer sausage to a bowl. Add the next five ingredients (through paprika) to the pot. Cook and stir 30 seconds. Add chicken stock, water, and rice. Bring to boiling; reduce heat. Simmer, covered, 30 minutes.
**2.** Return sausage to pot. Stir in frozen vegetables, collard greens (if using), kidney beans, and undrained tomatoes. Return to boiling; reduce heat. Simmer, covered, about 5 minutes more or until rice is tender and collards are wilted. If using spinach, stir in just before serving.

**PER SERVING** (1⅔ cups each) **CAL** 255, **FAT** 5 g (1 g sat. fat), **CHOL** 22 mg, **SODIUM** 599 mg, **CARB** 35 g (11 g fiber, 10 g sugars), **PRO** 14 g

# 4

# MAIN-DISH
# MASTERPIECES

Think outside the roaster. You can serve a festive meal without a roast turkey. Enjoy succulent beef roast, all-in-one sheet-pan dinners, and specialty seafood entrées. You can even break out the grill for entertaining-special plank-smoked salmon and grilled chicken. If you do roast a turkey, you'll find some ideas for leftovers.

Panko-Crusted Beef Roast
with Hasselback Zucchini

## Panko-Crusted Beef Roast with Hasselback Zucchini

**15 g CARB**

**SERVES** 10
**HANDS ON** 25 min.
**TOTAL** 2 hr. 25 min.

1 3-lb. boneless beef round tip roast, trimmed
¾ tsp. sea salt
2 Tbsp. Dijon mustard
2 to 3 tsp. fennel seeds, crushed
2 Tbsp. panko bread crumbs
1½ lb. baby Dutch potatoes
4 Tbsp. olive oil
¾ tsp. garlic powder
½ cup grated Parmesan cheese
1 tsp. snipped fresh oregano
¼ tsp. black pepper
4 small or 2 large zucchini
1 recipe Mustard Sauce

**1.** Preheat oven to 325°F. Sprinkle meat with ¼ tsp. of the salt. Brush with mustard and sprinkle with fennel seeds. Press panko onto meat.
**2.** Place meat on a rack in a shallow roasting pan. Roast 1¾ to 2 hours for medium rare (135°F) or 2¼ to 2½ hours for medium (150°F).
**3.** Meanwhile, halve any large potatoes; place potatoes in a large bowl. Drizzle with 2 Tbsp. of the oil and sprinkle with the remaining ½ tsp. of the salt and ¼ tsp. of the garlic powder; toss to coat. Add potatoes to one side of roasting pan the last 1 hour of roasting.

**4.** Wipe out large bowl. In bowl combine cheese, oregano, pepper, and remaining ½ tsp. garlic powder. Cut zucchini crosswise into ½-inch slices, cutting almost to other side. Stuff cheese mixture between slices; drizzle with remaining 2 Tbsp. oil. Add zucchini to other side of roasting pan the last 30 minutes of roasting.
**5.** Remove from oven. Cover meat with foil; let stand 15 minutes. The temperature of the meat will rise 5°F to 10°F during standing. (If potatoes and zucchini are not tender, return to oven 10 to 15 minutes more or until tender.) Thinly slice meat. Serve with potatoes, zucchini, and Mustard Sauce.

**Mustard Sauce** In a bowl stir together ½ cup **light sour cream,** ⅓ cup **Dijon mustard,** 1 Tbsp. **olive oil,** and ¼ tsp. **black pepper.**

PER SERVING *(4 oz. meat + about 3 potatoes + ⅓ small zucchini + 1½ Tbsp. sauce each)* **CAL** 315, **FAT** 14 g (4 g sat. fat), **CHOL** 88 mg, **SODIUM** 592 mg, **CARB** 15 g (2 g fiber, 2 g sugars), **PRO** 32 g

## Balsamic Marinated Flank Steak on Shaved Parmesan Asparagus

**4 g CARB**

**SERVES** 4
**HANDS ON** 30 min.
**TOTAL** 1 hr. 10 min.

1 lb. beef flank steak
⅓ cup balsamic vinegar
2 tsp. packed brown sugar*
3 cloves garlic, minced
½ tsp. salt
½ tsp. dried Italian seasoning, crushed
1 lb. fresh thick asparagus spears, trimmed
1 lemon
2 tsp. olive oil
¼ cup shredded Parmesan cheese
¼ tsp. cracked black pepper

**1.** Trim fat from steak. Score steak on both sides with shallow cuts at 1-inch intervals in a diamond pattern. Place steak in a resealable plastic bag set in a shallow dish. For marinade, combine vinegar, brown sugar, two cloves garlic, ¼ tsp. of the salt, and the Italian seasoning. Pour over steak; seal bag. Marinate in the refrigerator 30 minutes to 2 hours, turning bag occasionally.
**2.** Meanwhile, remove 1 tsp. zest and squeeze 1 Tbsp. juice from lemon; place in a large bowl. Add olive oil, remaining garlic clove, and ¼ tsp. salt. Whisk to combine. Using a vegetable peeler, cut asparagus into thin ribbons; add to bowl with the dressing. Toss to combine.
**3.** Drain steak; discard marinade. Grill steak, uncovered, over medium until desired doneness, turning once. Allow 17 to 21 minutes for medium (160°F). Thinly slice steak. Spoon asparagus mixture onto a platter. Sprinkle with Parmesan and pepper. Top with steak.

PER SERVING *(3 oz. meat + 1 cup asparagus each)* **CAL** 236, **FAT** 12 g (5 g sat. fat), **CHOL** 77 mg, **SODIUM** 318 mg, **CARB** 4 g (1 g fiber, 2 g sugars), **PRO** 27 g

*Sugar Sub Choose Splenda Brown Sugar Blend. Follow package directions to use 2 tsp. equivalent.

**PER SERVING WITH SUB** Same as above.

« **QUICK TIP** To prevent slicing all the way through zucchini, arrange chopsticks or wooden spoons lengthwise on opposite sides of zucchini. Cut zucchini into slices, stopping when the knife reaches the chopsticks.

Balsamic Marinated
Flank Steak on Shaved
Parmesan Asparagus
*recipe, p. 63*

**QUICK TIP** If you have thin asparagus spears, quarter them lengthwise instead of peeling them into ribbons.

**Beef and Sweet Potato Pan Roast**

## Beef and Sweet Potato Pan Roast

| **27g** CARB | **SERVES** 4 |
| --- | --- |
| | **HANDS ON** 15 min. |
| | **TOTAL** 55 min. |

Nonstick cooking spray
- 2 Tbsp. olive oil
- 2 tsp. dried Italian seasoning, crushed
- 4 cloves garlic, minced
- ½ tsp. salt
- ¼ tsp. crushed red pepper
- 1 lb. medium sweet potatoes, peeled if desired and cut into 1-inch wedges
- 2 8-oz. beef shoulder petite tenders
- 1 cup cherry tomatoes
- 1 recipe Chopped Parsley Topping

**1.** Preheat oven to 450°F. Coat a shallow roasting pan with cooking spray. In a small bowl combine oil, Italian seasoning, garlic, salt, and crushed red pepper. Place sweet potatoes in prepared roasting pan. Add half of the oil mixture; toss to coat. Roast 10 minutes. Meanwhile, spread remaining oil mixture over beef.
**2.** Stir sweet potatoes and push to edges of roasting pan. Place meat in center of pan. Roast 5 minutes. Add tomatoes; roast 10 to 15 minutes more or until desired doneness (135°F for medium rare or 150°F for medium). Remove from oven. Cover meat with foil; let stand 15 minutes. The temperature of the meat will rise 5°F to 10°F during standing. Before serving, sprinkle with Chopped Parsley Topping.

**Chopped Parsley Topping** In a small bowl stir together **¼ cup snipped fresh parsley; 2 tsp. orange zest; 2 cloves garlic, minced;** and **⅛ tsp. salt**.

**PER SERVING** *(3 oz. meat + ¾ cup sweet potatoes each)* **CAL** 335, **FAT** 14 g (3 g sat. fat), **CHOL** 64 mg, **SODIUM** 487 mg, **CARB** 27 g (4 g fiber, 6 g sugars), **PRO** 26 g

**Pork Roast**

Tip Look for beef shoulder petite tenders that are similar in shape to pork tenderloin but smaller. Don't choose those that are labeled as medallions or slices.

**Beef Tenderloin and Sweet Potato Pan Roast** Substitute **one 1-lb. center-cut beef tenderloin roast** for the beef tenders. Prepare as directed, except do not roast sweet potatoes before adding meat. Place tenderloin in center of prepared roasting pan. Roast 30 to 35 minutes for medium rare (135°F) or 40 to 45 minutes for medium (150°F), adding sweet potatoes the last 25 minutes and tomatoes the last 10 minutes. Cover meat with foil; let stand 15 minutes. Serve as directed.

PER SERVING Same as original, except **CAL** 343, **FAT** 15 g (4 g sat. fat), **CHOL** 69 mg, **PRO** 27 g

## Pork Roast

**18 g**
**CARB**

| | |
|---|---|
| **SERVES** | 8 |
| **HANDS ON** | 20 min. |
| **TOTAL** | 1 hr. 30 min. |

- ¼ cup olive oil
- 2 Tbsp. snipped fresh rosemary
- 2 Tbsp. snipped fresh thyme
- 6 cloves garlic, minced
- 1 tsp. salt
- ½ tsp. black pepper
- 1 lb. tiny new potatoes, halved
- ½ of a 1½-lb. butternut squash, peeled, seeded, and cut into 1½-inch pieces
- 3 medium carrots and/or parsnips, peeled, halved lengthwise, and cut into 2-inch pieces
- 1 large onion, cut into wedges
- 1 2- to 2½-lb. boneless pork top loin roast (single loin), trimmed of fat

**1.** Preheat oven to 450°F. In a small bowl combine first six ingredients (through pepper). Place potatoes, squash, carrots, and onion in a large roasting pan. Drizzle with half of the rosemary mixture; toss to coat. Push vegetables to edges of pan.

**2.** Spread remaining rosemary mixture over meat; place in center of pan. Roast 20 to 25 minutes or until meat is beginning to brown.

**3.** Reduce oven temperature to 350°F. Roast 40 to 45 minutes more or until a thermometer registers 145°F and vegetables are tender, stirring vegetables occasionally. Remove from oven. Cover meat and vegetables with foil; let stand 10 minutes before serving.

PER SERVING *(4 oz. meat + ¾ cup vegetables each)* **CAL** 285, **FAT** 11 g (2 g sat. fat), **CHOL** 71 mg, **SODIUM** 363 mg, **CARB** 18 g (3 g fiber, 3 g sugars), **PRO** 27 g

**QUICK TIP** If the polenta becomes too thick while standing, stir in additional water to reach desired consistency.

## Mexican-Spiced Pork with Cheddar-Jalapeño Polenta

**32 g**
**CARB**

**SERVES** 4
**TOTAL** 25 min.

- 4 tsp. olive oil
- ½ cup chopped onion
- 1 fresh jalapeño chile pepper, seeded and minced (tip, *p. 156*)
- 2 cups no-salt-added chicken broth
- ½ cup quick-cooking polenta mix
- ¾ cup shredded reduced-fat cheddar cheese (3 oz.)
- 2 tsp. chili powder
- ½ tsp. garlic powder
- ½ tsp. ground cumin
- ¼ tsp. dried oregano, crushed
- ¼ tsp. ground coriander
- ¼ tsp. black pepper
- ⅛ tsp. salt
- 1 1-lb. pork tenderloin
  Snipped fresh cilantro (optional)

**1.** For polenta, in a 2-qt. saucepan heat 2 tsp. of the oil over medium. Add onion and jalapeño pepper; cook and stir 5 minutes. Add broth. Bring to boiling. Gradually add polenta mix, stirring constantly. Reduce heat to low. Cook about 5 minutes or until thickened. Stir in cheese until melted. Remove from heat; cover and keep warm.
**2.** In a small bowl stir together the next seven ingredients (through salt).
**3.** Trim fat from meat. Cut meat crosswise into eight pieces. Using the flat side of a meat mallet, flatten pieces between two pieces of plastic wrap to about ½ inch thick. Sprinkle spice mixture evenly over meat; rub in with your fingers.
**4.** In a 12-inch nonstick skillet heat the remaining 2 tsp. oil over medium-high. Add meat; cook about 5 minutes or until browned but still slightly pink in center, turning once. Serve meat over polenta. If desired, sprinkle with cilantro.

**PER SERVING** (*2 pork medallions + ½ cup polenta each*) **CAL** 369, **FAT** 12 g (4 g sat. fat), **CHOL** 88 mg, **SODIUM** 355 mg, **CARB** 32 g (5 g fiber, 1 g sugars), **PRO** 34 g

## Hawaiian Pork

**42 g** CARB

**SERVES** 4
**HANDS ON** 25 min.
**TOTAL** 40 min.

Nonstick cooking spray
1 1-lb. pork tenderloin, trimmed
2 Tbsp. olive oil
¼ tsp. kosher salt
¼ tsp. black pepper
3 Tbsp. reduced-sodium soy sauce
2 Tbsp. honey
1 Tbsp. lime juice
1 Tbsp. grated fresh ginger
4 cloves garlic, minced
1 tsp. paprika
¼ tsp. ground cumin
¼ tsp. ground coriander
2 cups 1-inch chunks peeled fresh pineapple
1 cup red sweet pepper strips
6 Tbsp. 2-inch pieces green onions
1 8.8-oz. pouch cooked whole grain brown rice
¼ cup snipped fresh cilantro

**1.** Preheat oven to 425°F. Coat a 15×10-inch baking pan with cooking spray. Place meat in the prepared baking pan. Drizzle with 1 Tbsp. of the oil and sprinkle with salt and black pepper. Roast 10 minutes.
**2.** Meanwhile, in a small bowl combine the next eight ingredients (through coriander). In a medium bowl combine the remaining 1 Tbsp. oil, pineapple, sweet pepper, and green onions.
**3.** Arrange pineapple mixture around meat in pan; drizzle meat and pineapple mixture with soy mixture. Roast 15 minutes more or until meat registers 145°F. Remove from oven. Let meat stand 3 minutes before slicing.
**4.** Microwave rice according to package directions. Serve rice with meat and pineapple mixture. Top with cilantro.

**PER SERVING** (*3 oz. meat + ¾ cup rice mixture each*) **CAL** 373, **FAT** 11 g (2 g sat. fat), **CHOL** 74 mg, **SODIUM** 555 mg, **CARB** 42 g (4 g fiber, 19 g sugars), **PRO** 28 g

Hawaiian Pork

**Maple-Roasted Chicken Thighs with Sweet Potatoes and Brussels Sprouts**

## Maple-Roasted Chicken Thighs with Sweet Potatoes and Brussels Sprouts

**45 g** | **SERVES** 4
**CARB** | **HANDS ON** 20 min.
| **TOTAL** 50 min.

2 Tbsp. pure maple syrup
4 tsp. olive oil
1 Tbsp. snipped fresh thyme
½ tsp. salt
½ tsp. black pepper
1 lb. sweet potatoes, peeled and cut into 1-inch wedges
1 lb. Brussels sprouts, trimmed and halved
Nonstick cooking spray
4 bone-in chicken thighs (1¼ lb. total), skinned
3 Tbsp. chopped pecans, toasted
3 Tbsp. snipped dried cranberries

1. Preheat oven to 425°F. In a small bowl combine maple syrup, 1 tsp. of the oil, the thyme, and ¼ tsp. each of the salt and pepper. In a large bowl combine sweet potatoes and Brussels sprouts. Drizzle with the remaining 3 tsp. oil and sprinkle with the remaining ¼ tsp. each salt and pepper; toss to coat.
2. Line a 15×10-inch baking pan with foil. Heat prepared pan in oven 5 minutes. Remove pan from oven and coat with cooking spray. Arrange chicken, meaty sides down, in center of pan. Arrange vegetables around chicken. Roast 15 minutes.
3. Turn chicken and vegetables; brush with maple syrup mixture. Roast about 15 minutes more or until chicken is done (at least 175°F) and potatoes are tender. Serve topped with pecans and cranberries.

**PER SERVING** (1 chicken thigh + 4 sweet potato wedges + ¾ cup Brussels sprouts each) **CAL** 436, **FAT** 14 g (3 g sat. fat), **CHOL** 133 mg, **SODIUM** 491 mg, **CARB** 45 g (9 g fiber, 18 g sugars), **PRO** 34 g

## Chicken Parmesan with Broccolini

**24 g** | **SERVES** 2
**CARB** | **TOTAL** 30 min.

2 Tbsp. refrigerated egg product
½ cup whole wheat panko bread crumbs
⅛ tsp. salt
Dash black pepper
1 8-oz. skinless, boneless chicken breast half, halved horizontally
Nonstick cooking spray
6 oz. trimmed Broccolini, large stems halved lengthwise
2 tsp. olive oil
½ cup roasted red sweet pepper
1 Tbsp. almonds, toasted
1 Tbsp. snipped fresh basil
2 tsp. lemon juice
1 clove garlic, minced
2 Tbsp. finely shredded Parmesan cheese

1. Preheat oven to 425°F. Pour egg into a shallow dish. In another shallow dish combine panko, salt, and black pepper. Dip chicken in egg, then in panko mixture, turning to coat. Place chicken in a 15×10-inch baking pan; lightly coat with cooking spray. Place Broccolini next to chicken; drizzle with oil. Bake about 15 minutes or until chicken is done (165°F).
2. Meanwhile, for sauce, in a food processor combine the next five ingredients (through garlic). Cover and process until smooth. Transfer to a small saucepan; heat through.
3. To serve, spoon sauce over chicken and Broccolini and top with cheese and, if desired, additional basil.

**PER SERVING** (3½ oz. chicken + 3 oz. broccolini + ¼ cup sauce each) **CAL** 345, **FAT** 12 g (2 g sat. fat), **CHOL** 86 mg, **SODIUM** 517 mg, **CARB** 24 g (5 g fiber, 4 g sugars), **PRO** 36 g

Chicken Parmesan
with Broccolini

## Chicken with Red Wine Pan Sauce

**3g**
**CARB**

**SERVES** 4
**TOTAL** 35 min.

- 4 4- to 5-oz. skinless, boneless chicken breast halves
- ¼ tsp. salt
- ¼ tsp. black pepper
- 2 Tbsp. butter
- 1 cup sliced mushrooms
- ⅔ cup red wine or reduced-sodium chicken broth + 1 Tbsp. red wine vinegar
- ½ cup reduced-sodium chicken broth
- 1 Tbsp. balsamic vinegar
- 2 tsp. snipped fresh thyme
- 2 tsp. snipped fresh parsley

**1.** Using the flat side of a meat mallet, flatten chicken between two pieces of plastic wrap to about ¼ inch thick. Sprinkle chicken with salt and pepper.
**2.** In a 12-inch skillet melt 1 Tbsp. of the butter over medium-high. Reduce heat to medium. Add chicken to skillet. Cook chicken 6 to 8 minutes or until no longer pink, turning once. Transfer chicken to a platter; cover with foil to keep warm. Turn off burner or remove skillet from heat.
**3.** Add mushrooms, wine, broth, vinegar, and thyme to the hot skillet. Return skillet to heat. Cook and stir to scrape up any browned bits from bottom of pan. Bring to boiling. Boil gently, uncovered, about 8 minutes or until liquid is slightly thickened and reduced. Reduce heat to medium-low.

**4.** Add remaining 1 Tbsp. butter and the parsley to skillet, stirring until butter is melted. Serve sauce over chicken.

**PER SERVING** *(1 chicken breast half + 2 Tbsp. pan sauce each)* **CAL** 225, **FAT** 9 g (4 g sat. fat), **CHOL** 88 mg, **SODIUM** 401 mg, **CARB** 3 g (0 g fiber, 1 g sugars), **PRO** 25 g

Chicken with
Red Wine Pan Sauce

## Chicken with Roquefort Sauce

**16 g CARB**

**SERVES** 2
**HANDS ON** 15 min.
**TOTAL** 30 min.

- ½ cup plain fat-free yogurt
- ¼ cup chopped red onion
- 2 Tbsp. crumbled Roquefort or other blue cheese
- 1 Tbsp. snipped fresh chives
- ⅛ tsp. white pepper
- 2 firm, yet ripe, small pears, halved lengthwise, cored, and stemmed
  Lemon juice
- 4 4-oz. skinless, boneless chicken breast halves
- ¼ tsp. salt
- ¼ tsp. black pepper

**1.** For sauce, in a bowl stir together the first five ingredients (through white pepper). Cover and refrigerate until ready to serve. Brush the cut sides of pear halves with lemon juice. Sprinkle chicken with salt and black pepper.
**2.** Grill chicken, covered, over medium 12 to 15 minutes or until done (165°F), turning once. Place pear halves, cut sides down, on grill rack next to chicken the last 5 minutes of grilling. Serve the chicken and pears with sauce.

**To Broil** Preheat broiler. Place chicken on the unheated rack of a broiler pan. Broil 4 to 5 inches from the heat 12 to 15 minutes or until done (165°F), turning once. Place pear halves, cut sides down, on broiler rack next to chicken the last 5 minutes of broiling.

**PER SERVING** (1 chicken breast half + ½ of a pear + 3 Tbsp. sauce each) **CAL** 214, **FAT** 3 g (1 g sat. fat), **CHOL** 69 mg, **SODIUM** 214 mg, **CARB** 16 g (2 g fiber, 11 g sugars), **PRO** 29 g

**Tip** If you can't find small chicken breast halves, cut two 8-oz. breast halves in half horizontally make four thin breast pieces.

**Chicken with Roquefort Sauce**

**CREAMY CHIVE DRESSING** In a bowl whisk together ½ cup low-fat buttermilk, ¼ cup light mayonnaise, 2 Tbsp. chopped fresh chives, ¼ tsp. salt, and ⅛ tsp. black pepper.

**Grilled Buttermilk Chicken and Rosemary Potatoes**

## Grilled Buttermilk Chicken and Rosemary Potatoes

**24 g**
**CARB**

| | |
|---|---|
| **SERVES** 4 | |
| **HANDS ON** 25 min. | |
| **TOTAL** 9 hr. | |

- 3 5-oz. skinless, boneless chicken breast halves
- ⅔ cup low-fat buttermilk
- 4 cloves garlic, minced
- 3 medium Yukon gold potatoes (12 oz. total), cut into ½-inch wedges
- 1 Tbsp. olive oil
- 2 tsp. chopped fresh rosemary or ½ tsp. dried rosemary, crushed
- 4 cups torn fresh butterhead lettuce
- 1 cup thinly sliced celery
- ¾ cup shredded carrots
- 1 recipe Creamy Chive Dressing

**1.** Place chicken breast halves in a resealable plastic bag set in a bowl. Add buttermilk, garlic, ½ tsp. *black pepper*, and ¼ tsp. *salt*. Seal bag; turn to coat chicken. Marinate chicken in the refrigerator 8 to 10 hours, turning occasionally.

**2.** Fold a 36×18-inch piece of heavy foil in half to make a double thickness of foil that measures 18×18 inches. Add potatoes to center of foil. Drizzle with oil; sprinkle with rosemary. Bring together two opposite edges of foil; seal with a double fold. Fold remaining edges together to enclose potatoes, leaving room for steam to build.

**3.** Place potato packet on a grill rack over medium. Grill, covered, 30 to 35 minutes or until potatoes are tender, turning packet occasionally. Drain chicken, discarding marinade. Add chicken to grill rack alongside potato packet. Grill, covered, 14 to 16 minutes or until done (165°F), turning once. Remove packet from grill; cool slightly before carefully opening packet to avoid steam.

**4.** Thinly slice chicken. Divide lettuce among four plates. Top with chicken, potatoes, celery, and carrots. Drizzle with Creamy Chive Dressing.

**PER SERVING** (2¼ cups salad + 3½ oz. chicken + 3 Tbsp. dressing each) **CAL** 318, **FAT** 11 g (2 g sat. fat), **CHOL** 90 mg, **SODIUM** 588 mg, **CARB** 24 g (4 g fiber, 7 g sugars), **PRO** 31 g

**Turkey-Vegetable Bake**

## Turkey-Vegetable Bake

**29 g**
**CARB**

| | |
|---|---|
| **SERVES** 6 | |
| **HANDS ON** 25 min. | |
| **TOTAL** 1 hr. 10 min. | |

- 2 cups sliced fresh mushrooms
- ¾ cup chopped red or yellow sweet pepper
- ½ cup chopped onion
- 2 cloves garlic, minced
- 2 Tbsp. light butter with canola oil
- ¼ cup all-purpose flour
- ¾ tsp. salt
- ½ tsp. dried thyme, crushed
- ¼ tsp. black pepper
- 2 cups fat-free milk
- 1 10-oz. pkg. frozen chopped spinach, thawed and well drained
- 2 cups cooked brown rice or white rice
- 2 cups chopped cooked turkey or chicken
- ½ cup finely shredded Parmesan cheese (2 oz.)

**1.** Preheat oven to 350°F. In a 12-inch skillet cook and stir mushrooms, sweet pepper, onion, and garlic in hot butter over medium until tender. Stir in flour, salt, thyme, and black pepper. Slowly stir in milk; cook and stir until thickened and bubbly. Stir in spinach, rice, turkey, and ¼ cup of the Parmesan cheese.

**2.** Spoon mixture into a 2-qt. rectangular baking dish. Sprinkle with remaining Parmesan cheese. Bake, covered, 20 minutes. Uncover and bake about 10 minutes more or until heated. Let stand 15 minutes before serving.

**PER SERVING** (1 cup each) **CAL** 275, **FAT** 6 g (3 g sat. fat), **CHOL** 55 mg, **SODIUM** 592 mg, **CARB** 29 g (3 g fiber, 6 g sugars), **PRO** 24 g

**Turkey-Cucumber Sandwiches with Citrus-Cilantro Spread**

## Turkey and Stuffing Skillet

**37 g**
**CARB**

**SERVES** 4
**HANDS ON** 20 min.
**TOTAL** 40 min.

4 Tbsp. butter
4 cups small broccoli florets
1 cup chopped onion
1 cup chopped celery
2 Tbsp. snipped fresh parsley
4 tsp. snipped fresh sage or ½ tsp. dried sage, crushed
½ tsp. black pepper
1 to 1½ cups unsalted chicken broth
6 oz. ciabatta or baguette-style French bread, cubed and dried
1 lb. boneless turkey breast tenderloin, cut into ¼-inch-thick slices
¼ cup dried cranberries
Snipped fresh parsley (optional)

**1.** In a 12-inch nonstick skillet melt 2 Tbsp. of the butter over medium-high. Add broccoli, onion, and celery. Cook and stir 5 to 6 minutes or until broccoli is crisp-tender. Stir in parsley, sage, and pepper. Add 1 cup of the broth; bring to boiling.
**2.** Place bread cubes in a large bowl; drizzle with the hot vegetable mixture. Toss lightly to combine. Cover and keep warm.
**3.** Place the remaining 2 Tbsp. butter in the skillet. Add meat; cook 4 to 5 minutes over medium-high or until no longer pink, turning once. Remove meat from skillet. Spread bread mixture evenly in skillet, adding the remaining ½ cup broth if needed to moisten. Top with cooked meat. Top with cranberries. Cover and heat. If desired, top with additional snipped fresh parsley.

**PER SERVING** (2 cups each) **CAL** 399, **FAT** 13 g (8 g sat. fat), **CHOL** 102 mg, **SODIUM** 392 mg, **CARB** 37 g (5 g fiber, 10 g sugars), **PRO** 36 g

## Turkey-Cucumber Sandwiches with Citrus-Cilantro Spread

**33 g**
**CARB**

**SERVES** 4
**TOTAL** 20 min.

1 small lemon
½ cup plain fat-free Greek yogurt
¼ cup snipped fresh cilantro
¼ cup reduced-fat feta cheese
¼ tsp. ground cumin
2 large whole grain naan bread, halved crosswise
1 cup lightly packed fresh baby spinach
8 oz. cooked turkey breast, thinly sliced
1 cup cucumber ribbons
6 Tbsp. thin slivers red onion

**1.** Remove ¼ tsp. zest and squeeze 2 tsp. juice from lemon. In a small bowl combine zest, juice, yogurt, cilantro, feta, and cumin.
**2.** Lay the naan bread on a flat surface. Top with spinach leaves. Carefully spread yogurt mixture over spinach. Top with turkey, cucumber, and red onion. Fold bread up around filling to serve.

**PER SERVING** (1 sandwich each) **CAL** 306, **FAT** 8 g (3 g sat. fat), **CHOL** 50 mg, **SODIUM** 571 mg, **CARB** 33 g (5 g fiber, 5 g sugars), **PRO** 27 g

Tip Use a vegetable peeler to cut cucumber lengthwise into thin ribbons.

Turkey and Stuffing Skillet

## Sausage- and Egg-Stuffed Acorn Squash

**46 g**
**CARB**

**SERVES** 2
**HANDS ON** 15 min.
**TOTAL** 55 min.

1 1-lb. acorn squash, halved lengthwise and seeded
¾ cup cooked turkey sausage crumbles
⅓ cup chopped onion
⅔ cup chopped red or green cooking apple
2 tsp. canola oil
¾ cup refrigerated or frozen egg product, thawed, or 3 eggs, lightly beaten
Dash salt
4 tsp. pure maple syrup
2 Tbsp. coarsely chopped pecans
Fresh sage (optional)

1. Preheat oven to 350°F. Line a 2-qt. rectangular baking dish with parchment paper or foil. Place squash halves, cut sides down, in the prepared dish. Bake 30 to 40 minutes or until tender.
2. Meanwhile, in a 10-inch nonstick skillet cook sausage and onion over medium-high about 3 minutes or until onion is tender. Add apple; cook 3 to 5 minutes more or until apple is tender, stirring frequently. Reduce heat to medium. Push sausage mixture from center of skillet. Pour oil into center; add egg. Cook, without stirring, until egg begins to set around edges. Continue to cook, stirring frequently, 1 to 2 minutes or until egg is cooked through. Stir egg into sausage mixture to combine.
3. Using a wide metal spatula, carefully turn squash halves cut sides up and sprinkle with salt. Brush tops and insides of cavities with 2 tsp. of the syrup. Fill with sausage mixture, pressing lightly to fit if needed. Sprinkle with pecans.
4. Bake about 10 minutes more or until stuffed squash is heated through and pecans are lightly toasted. Drizzle with the remaining 2 tsp. syrup and, if desired, top with sage.

**PER SERVING** (*1 stuffed squash half each*)
**CAL** 361, **FAT** 14 g (2 g sat. fat), **CHOL** 30 mg, **SODIUM** 614 mg, **CARB** 46 g (6 g fiber, 20 g sugars), **PRO** 19 g

Tip Turkey sausage crumbles are a great convenience product, but if you can't find them, cook a pound of fresh turkey sausage. Use ¾ cup for this recipe and freeze the rest in a resealable plastic freezer bag.

Sausage- and Egg-Stuffed Acorn Squash

**Plank-Smoked Salmon with Grilled-Pepper Relish**

## Plank-Smoked Salmon with Grilled-Pepper Relish

**5 g CARB**

**SERVES** 8
**HANDS ON** 25 min.
**TOTAL** 2 hr. 45 min.

- 1 2-lb. fresh or frozen salmon fillet with skin
- 1 grill plank (15×6½×⅜-inch), such as alder or cedar
- ¼ cup reduced-sodium soy sauce
- ¼ cup balsamic vinegar
- 3 Tbsp. honey
- 1 Tbsp. grated fresh ginger
- ½ tsp. crushed red pepper
- 3 red, yellow, and/or orange sweet peppers
- 3 Tbsp. thinly sliced fresh basil
- 2 Tbsp. chopped pitted Kalamata olives
- 2 tsp. olive oil
- 2 tsp. balsamic vinegar
- ¼ tsp. salt
- ¼ tsp. black pepper
- ¼ cup thinly bias-sliced green onions

1. Thaw salmon if frozen. Rinse salmon; pat dry. Soak plank in enough water to cover.
2. For marinade, in a bowl combine the next five ingredients (through crushed red pepper). Place salmon in a large resealable plastic bag set in a shallow dish. Pour marinade over salmon. Seal bag; turn to coat salmon. Marinate in the refrigerator 1 hour, turning bag occasionally. (Do not marinate longer.) Drain salmon, discarding marinade.
3. Grill sweet peppers, covered, over medium 10 to 12 minutes or until blistered and charred, turning occasionally. Wrap peppers in foil; let stand 15 minutes. Using a sharp knife, loosen edges of skins; gently pull off in strips and discard. Chop peppers into ½-inch pieces, discarding stems, seeds, and membranes.
4. Remove grill plank from water. Place plank on grill rack over medium heat. Grill, uncovered, 3 to 5 minutes or until plank begins to crackle and smoke. Place salmon, skin side down, on plank. Grill, covered, 18 to 22 minutes or until fish flakes easily.
5. Meanwhile, for relish, in a bowl stir together the chopped sweet peppers and the next six ingredients (through black pepper).
6. Sprinkle salmon with green onions and serve with relish.

**PER SERVING** (about 4 oz. salmon + 3 Tbsp. relish each) **CAL** 196, **FAT** 9 g (1 g sat. fat), **CHOL** 62 mg, **SODIUM** 197 mg, **CARB** 5 g (1 g fiber, 3 g sugars), **PRO** 23 g

Tip Look for grill planks in the grilling supplies section of hardware and home supply stores.

**QUICK TIP** If using carrots and/or green beans, precook them. In a covered medium saucepan cook the carrots and/or green beans in a small amount of boiling water 2 minutes. Drain.

**Salmon in Parchment Paper**

## Salmon in Parchment Paper

**13 g**
**CARB**

**SERVES** 4

**HANDS ON** 30 min.

**TOTAL** 55 min.

- 1 lb. fresh or frozen skinless salmon or halibut fillets, ¾ to 1 inch thick
- 4 cups fresh vegetables (such as sliced carrots; trimmed fresh green beans; sliced zucchini or yellow summer squash; sliced fresh mushrooms; and/or sliced red, yellow, and/or green sweet peppers)
- ½ cup sliced green onions
- 1 Tbsp. snipped fresh oregano or 1 tsp. dried oregano, crushed
- 2 tsp. orange zest
- ¼ tsp. salt
- ¼ tsp. black pepper
- 4 cloves garlic, halved
- 4 tsp. olive oil
- 1 medium orange, halved and thinly sliced
- 4 sprigs fresh oregano (optional)

**1.** Preheat oven to 350°F. Thaw fish if frozen. Rinse fish; pat dry. If necessary, cut into four serving-size pieces. Tear off four 14-inch squares of parchment paper. In a large bowl combine the next seven ingredients (through garlic); toss gently.

**2.** Divide vegetable mixture among the four pieces of parchment, placing vegetables on one side of each parchment square. Place one fish piece on top of each vegetable portion. Drizzle 1 tsp. of the oil over each fish piece. Top with orange slices. Fold parchment over fish and vegetables; fold in the open sides several times to secure, curving the edge into a circular pattern. Place parchment packets in a single layer in a 15×10-inch baking pan.

**3.** Bake 25 to 30 minutes or until fish flakes easily. Cut an "X" in the top of a parchment packet to check doneness; open carefully (steam will escape). If desired, top with fresh oregano sprigs.

**PER SERVING** (1 packet each) **CAL** 262, **FAT** 12 g (2 g sat. fat), **CHOL** 62 mg, **SODIUM** 359 mg, **CARB** 13 g (4 g fiber, 8 g sugars), **PRO** 25 g

## Baked Salmon with Cranberry Couscous

**32 g**
**CARB**

**SERVES** 4

**HANDS ON** 20 min.

**TOTAL** 1 hr.

- 4 4- to 5-oz. fresh or frozen skinless salmon fillets
- 1 orange
- 2 cups 1-inch pieces fresh thick asparagus spears
- ¾ cup low-sodium chicken broth, warmed
- ⅔ cup dry whole wheat couscous
- 2 Tbsp. dried cranberries, chopped
- 4 garlic cloves
- ¾ tsp. salt
- ⅛ tsp. crushed red pepper
- 1 tsp. snipped fresh rosemary
  Sliced green onions (optional)

**1.** Preheat oven to 450°F. Thaw fish if frozen. Rinse fish; pat dry. Remove zest and squeeze 3 Tbsp. juice from orange. In a 2-qt. rectangular baking dish combine the asparagus, broth, couscous, ½ tsp. of the orange zest, the orange juice, cranberries, half of the garlic, ½ tsp. of the salt, and the crushed red pepper.

**2.** Nestle salmon into couscous mixture. Top salmon with remaining garlic, salt, the rosemary, and, if desired, additional orange zest.

**3.** Bake, covered, about 30 minutes or until couscous is tender and fish flakes easily. Gently fluff couscous with a fork and, if desired, sprinkle with green onions.

**PER SERVING** (1 salmon fillet + ½ cup couscous mixture each) **CAL** 313, **FAT** 8 g (1 g sat. fat), **CHOL** 62 mg, **SODIUM** 504 mg, **CARB** 32 g (3 g fiber, 5 g sugars), **PRO** 29 g

Baked Salmon with Cranberry Couscous

Lemon-Roasted Tuna
and Asparagus

## Lemon-Roasted Tuna and Asparagus

**5g** **CARB**

| | |
|---|---|
| **SERVES** 4 | |
| **TOTAL** 20 min. | |

2 lemons
3 Tbsp. olive oil
½ tsp. black pepper
¼ tsp. salt
4 4-oz. fresh tuna steaks, cut ¾ inch thick
12 oz. asparagus spears, trimmed
1 5-oz. pkg. mixed baby salad greens
⅓ cup shaved Parmesan cheese (optional)

**1.** Preheat oven to 450°F. Remove 2 tsp. zest and squeeze juice from one of the lemons. For dressing, in a small bowl whisk together lemon zest and juice, oil, pepper, and salt. Cut remaining lemon into wedges.
**2.** Rinse fish; pat dry. In a 15×10-inch baking pan arrange fish and asparagus. Brush with 2 to 3 Tbsp. of the dressing. Roast 6 to 8 minutes or just until fish flakes and asparagus is crisp-tender.
**3.** Drizzle salad greens with the remaining dressing; toss to coat. If desired, sprinkle fish and asparagus with cheese. Serve with salad greens and lemon wedges.

**PER SERVING** *(4 oz. tuna + 4 or 5 pieces asparagus + ½ cup salad each)* **CAL** 234, **FAT** 11 g (2 g sat. fat), **CHOL** 44 mg, **SODIUM** 204 mg, **CARB** 5 g (2 g fiber, 2 g sugars), **PRO** 29 g

**Crispy Smoked
Fish Roll-Ups**

## Crispy Smoked Fish Roll-Ups

**16 g**
CARB

**SERVES** 4
**HANDS ON** 20 min.
**TOTAL** 40 min.

- 4 4-oz. fresh or frozen tilapia, flounder, or sole fillets
  Nonstick cooking spray
- 3 oz. thinly sliced smoked salmon (lox-style), cut into thin strips
- ¼ cup snipped fresh chives
- 2 Tbsp. finely chopped red onion
- 1 tsp. lemon zest
- ½ cup refrigerated or frozen egg product, thawed, or 2 eggs, lightly beaten
- 1 cup whole wheat or white panko bread crumbs
  Lemon wedges

1. Thaw fish if frozen. Preheat oven to 425°F. Coat a 2-qt. square baking dish with cooking spray.
2. Rinse fish; pat dry. Place smoked salmon on top of fish. Sprinkle with chives, onion, and lemon zest. Roll up fish and, if needed, secure with wooden toothpicks.
3. Pour egg into a shallow dish. Place bread crumbs in another shallow dish. Dip fish rolls into egg, then into crumbs, turning to coat. Arrange in the prepared baking dish; lightly coat tops of fish rolls with cooking spray.
4. Bake 18 to 20 minutes or until tops are light brown and fish flakes easily. Top with additional chives and/or lemon zest (if desired) and serve with lemon wedges.

**PER SERVING** (1 roll-up each) **CAL** 224, **FAT** 3 g (1 g sat. fat), **CHOL** 66 mg, **SODIUM** 350 mg, **CARB** 16 g (2 g fiber, 1 g sugars), **PRO** 33 g

**Lemon-Garlic Shrimp over Orzo with Zucchini**

## Lemon-Garlic Shrimp over Orzo with Zucchini

**30 g**
CARB

**SERVES** 4
**TOTAL** 40 min.

- 1½ lb. fresh or frozen large shrimp in shells
- 2 lemons
- ¾ cup dried orzo pasta
- 2 Tbsp. olive oil
- 1 Tbsp. unsalted butter
- 3 cloves garlic, minced
- ½ tsp. salt
- ⅛ tsp. crushed red pepper
- 2 cups sliced zucchini
- ¼ cup thinly sliced shallots
- ¼ tsp. black pepper
- 2 Tbsp. water
- 1 tsp. snipped fresh rosemary
- 2 Tbsp. snipped fresh dill

1. Thaw shrimp if frozen. Peel and devein shrimp, leaving tails intact if desired. Rinse shrimp; pat dry. Using a vegetable peeler, remove zest from one of the lemons and cut into thin slivers. Squeeze ¼ cup juice from 1½ lemons. Set the remaining lemon half aside.

2. Cook orzo according to package directions, omitting any salt and fat; drain.
3. In a 10-inch nonstick skillet heat 1 Tbsp. of the oil and the butter over medium-high. Add shrimp, two of the garlic cloves, ¼ tsp. of the salt, and the crushed red pepper. Cook and stir about 2 minutes or just until shrimp are opaque. Stir in 2 Tbsp. of the lemon juice. Remove mixture from skillet; cover to keep warm.
4. In skillet heat the remaining 1 Tbsp. oil over medium-high. Add zucchini, shallots, pepper, and the remaining garlic clove and ¼ tsp. salt. Cook 3 to 4 minutes or until zucchini is light brown, stirring occasionally. Add the water, rosemary, and the remaining 2 Tbsp. lemon juice, stirring to scrape up any browned bits. Stir in cooked orzo; heat through.
5. Stir shrimp mixture into orzo mixture and sprinkle with dill and lemon slivers. Squeeze juice from the reserved lemon half over mixture.

**PER SERVING** (¾ cup shrimp mixture + ¾ cup orzo mixture each) **CAL** 355, **FAT** 11 g (3 g sat. fat), **CHOL** 246 mg, **SODIUM** 476 mg, **CARB** 30 g (2 g fiber, 4 g sugars), **PRO** 35 g

Curried Shrimp
with Cauliflower
and Chickpeas

## Curried Shrimp with Cauliflower and Chickpeas

**40 g**
CARB

| | |
|---|---|
| **SERVES** 8 | |
| **HANDS ON** 20 min. | |
| **SLOW COOK** 5 hr. 30 min. | |

- 5 cups cauliflower florets
- 1 large onion, cut into ½-inch wedges
- 1 cup ¼-inch slices carrots
- 1 cup reduced-sodium chicken broth
- ½ cup sliced celery
- 2 Tbsp. curry powder
- 1 tsp. salt
- ¼ tsp. cayenne pepper
- 2 lb. fresh or frozen medium shrimp in shells
- 2 15-oz. cans no-salt-added garbanzo beans (chickpeas), rinsed and drained
- 1 cup canned unsweetened light coconut milk
- 2⅔ cups cooked brown basmati rice
- ½ cup snipped fresh cilantro
- ½ cup chopped unsalted dry-roasted peanuts
  Lime wedges

**1.** In a 5- to 6-qt. slow cooker combine the first eight ingredients (through cayenne pepper). Cover and cook on low 5 to 6 hours or high 2½ to 3 hours.
**2.** Meanwhile, thaw shrimp if frozen. Peel and devein shrimp, leaving tails intact if desired. Rinse shrimp; pat dry. Cover and chill until needed.
**3.** If using low, turn to high. Stir shrimp, beans, and coconut milk into mixture in cooker. Cover and cook 30 minutes more.
**4.** Serve shrimp mixture over rice. Sprinkle with cilantro and peanuts and serve with lime wedges.

**PER SERVING** (1⅓ cups shrimp mixture + ⅓ cup rice each) **CAL** 337, **FAT** 8 g (2 g sat. fat), **CHOL** 159 mg, **SODIUM** 528 mg, **CARB** 40 g (8 g fiber, 4 g sugars), **PRO** 30 g

## Orange Pistachio-Stuffed Grilled Scallops

**18 g**
CARB

| | |
|---|---|
| **SERVES** 4 | |
| **HANDS ON** 30 min. | |
| **TOTAL** 40 min. | |

- 12 fresh or frozen large sea scallops (1 to 1¼ lb. total)
- 1 small fennel bulb
- 2 oranges
- 3 Tbsp. olive oil
- 2 Tbsp. snipped fresh Italian parsley
- 1 Tbsp. finely chopped pistachio nuts
- 1 Tbsp. sherry vinegar or white balsamic vinegar
- 2 tsp. honey
- ¼ tsp. salt
- ¼ tsp. black pepper
- 4 cups arugula

**1.** Thaw scallops if frozen. Rinse scallops; pat dry. Make a horizontal cut through the center of each scallop, cutting almost to, but not through, the opposite side. Chill scallops until needed.
**2.** Cut off and discard fennel stalks, reserving fennel fronds. Remove any wilted outer layers from bulb; cut a thin slice from the base. Cut bulb lengthwise into quarters; cut core out of each quarter. Snip 2 Tbsp. of the fronds.
**3.** Remove 1 tsp. zest from one of the oranges. Working over a bowl to catch the juice, use a small sharp knife to peel and section oranges. Reserve 1 Tbsp. of the juice.
**4.** For gremolata, in a bowl combine the 2 Tbsp. fennel fronds, the 1 tsp. orange zest, 1 Tbsp. of the oil, the parsley, and the pistachios. For vinaigrette, in a screw-top jar combine the 1 Tbsp. orange juice, the remaining 2 Tbsp. oil, the vinegar, honey, and ⅛ tsp. each of the salt and pepper. Cover and shake well.
**5.** Lightly grease a large grill pan. Stuff scallops with gremolata and secure with wooden toothpicks if necessary. Reserve any remaining gremolata. Lightly brush scallops with additional olive oil and sprinkle with remaining

**Orange Pistachio-Stuffed Grilled Scallops**

⅛ tsp. each salt and pepper. Place scallops in the prepared grill pan.
**6.** Place grill pan with scallops and the fennel on the grill rack. Grill, covered, over medium-high 11 to 14 minutes or until scallops are opaque and fennel is tender and lightly charred, turning once. Remove toothpicks from scallops. Slice fennel.
**7.** Serve scallops on arugula with fennel and orange sections. Sprinkle with any remaining gremolata and drizzle with vinaigrette. If desired, sprinkle with additional chopped pistachios.

**PER SERVING** (3 scallops + 1 cup arugula + ½ orange + ¼ fennel bulb each) **CAL** 260, **FAT** 12 g (2 g sat. fat), **CHOL** 37 mg, **SODIUM** 364 mg, **CARB** 18 g (3 g fiber, 11 g sugars), **PRO** 21 g

Mushroom-Farro
Melanzane

**QUICK TIP** If you can't find precooked farro, make your own. Combine 2 cups water and ⅔ cup pearled farro in a saucepan. Bring to boiling. Simmer, covered, about 30 minutes or until tender. Drain if necessary.

## Mushroom-Farro Melanzane

**27 g**
**CARB**

**SERVES** 6
**HANDS ON** 30 min.
**TOTAL** 50 min.

- 1 small eggplant, trimmed and sliced ½ inch thick
- 3 Tbsp. olive oil
- 2 cups sliced fresh cremini mushrooms
- ¾ cup chopped shallots
- 4 cloves garlic, minced
- 1 8-oz. pkg. precooked farro
- 1½ cups tomato puree
- 2 small zucchini, halved lengthwise and thinly sliced
- 1 cup cherry tomatoes, halved
- ¼ cup dry red wine or water
- 2 Tbsp. snipped fresh oregano
- 1½ cups shredded Italian cheese blend
- 2 tsp. snipped fresh thyme
- ½ tsp. sea salt
- ¼ tsp. black pepper
  Snipped fresh oregano (optional)

**1.** Brush eggplant slices with 2 Tbsp. of the oil. In a 10-inch broilerproof skillet cook eggplant in batches over medium until browned, turning once. Remove from skillet.

**2.** Add remaining 1 Tbsp. oil to skillet; heat over medium. Add mushrooms, shallots, and garlic; cook 6 to 8 minutes or until mushrooms are tender and light brown, stirring occasionally. Stir in next six ingredients (through oregano); stir in ¾ cup of the cheese. Top with eggplant slices, overlapping as needed. Sprinkle with remaining ¾ cup cheese, the thyme, salt, and pepper. Cook, covered, about 7 minutes or until heated and cheese is melted.

**3.** If desired, preheat broiler. Uncover skillet and broil 3 to 4 inches from heat about 1 minute or until cheese is golden and bubbly. If desired, sprinkle with additional oregano.

**PER SERVING** *(1¾ cups each)* **CAL** 277, **FAT** 14 g (5 g sat. fat), **CHOL** 20 mg, **SODIUM** 555 mg, **CARB** 27 g (5 g fiber, 8 g sugars), **PRO** 12 g

## Ratatouille

**9g** CARB

**SERVES** 6
**HANDS ON** 20 min.
**TOTAL** 40 min.

- ½ cup chopped onion
- 3 cloves garlic, minced
- 1 Tbsp. olive oil or canola oil
- 2 medium zucchini and/or yellow summer squash, halved lengthwise and cut into ¼-inch slices (about 4 cups)
- 1 12-oz. eggplant, peeled if desired and cut into 1-inch cubes (about 3 cups)
- 1½ cups chopped tomatoes, peeled if desired
- ¾ cup chopped green, red, and/or yellow sweet pepper
- 3 Tbsp. dry white wine, chicken broth, or vegetable broth
- ½ tsp. salt
- ¼ tsp. black pepper
- 1 Tbsp. snipped fresh basil or oregano

**1.** In a 10-inch skillet cook onion and garlic in hot oil over medium until onion is tender. Stir in the next seven ingredients (through black pepper). Bring to boiling; reduce heat. Simmer, covered, about 10 minutes or until vegetables are tender, stirring occasionally. Uncover and cook 10 minutes more or until most has evaporated, stirring occasionally. Just before serving, stir in basil.

**PER SERVING** (about 1 cup each) **CAL** 69, **FAT** 3 g (0 g sat. fat), **CHOL** 0 mg, **SODIUM** 205 mg, **CARB** 9 g (3 g fiber, 6 g sugars), **PRO** 2 g

**Ratatouille Casserole** Preheat oven to 375°F. In a bowl stir together **one 10.75-oz. can tomato puree, 2 Tbsp. balsamic vinegar, 2 Tbsp. dry white wine, 1 Tbsp. chopped fresh basil, 3 cloves minced garlic,** and **¼ tsp. each salt** and **black pepper.** Spoon mixture into a 2-qt. rectangular baking dish. Slice **½ of a medium onion** and separate into rings. Slice **2 medium zucchini, one 12-oz. eggplant,** and **3 roma tomatoes** into ¼-inch slices. Cut **1 small sweet pepper** into rings and halve the rings. Halve any large eggplant slices. Alternate vegetables in rows in the dish; brush with **1 Tbsp. olive oil** and sprinkle with **¼ tsp. each salt** and **black pepper.** Bake, uncovered, about 1 hour or until vegetables are tender. Let stand 10 minutes. Top with **fresh basil leaves.**

**PER SERVING** (⅙ recipe each) **CAL** 95, **FAT** 3 g (0 g sat. fat), **CHOL** 0 mg, **SODIUM** 260 mg, **CARB** 16 g (5 g fiber, 9 g sugars), **PRO** 3 g

Ratatouille

# 5

# SEASONAL
# SIDES & SALADS

Festive main dishes deserve equally special accompaniments.

Roasted root vegetables, hearty winter greens, and even everyday

basics like broccoli and cauliflower get light and flavorful

treatments. A sprinkle of bacon or drizzle of maple syrup adds the

right touch to take sides and salads from ordinary to extraordinary.

Asparagus in
Mustard-Dill
Sauce

## Asparagus in Mustard-Dill Sauce

**9g** CARB

**SERVES** 8
**TOTAL** 25 min.

4 lb. fresh asparagus spears
½ cup reduced-sodium chicken broth
¼ cup dill mustard
2 Tbsp. snipped fresh dill
   Black pepper

**1.** Preheat oven to 425°F. Snap off and discard woody bases from asparagus. Arrange asparagus in a 3-qt. rectangular baking dish. In a bowl stir together broth and mustard. Pour over asparagus, turning to coat.
**2.** Bake 15 to 20 minutes or until asparagus is crisp-tender. Sprinkle with dill and pepper.

**PER SERVING** (¾ cup each) **CAL** 46, **FAT** 0 g, **CHOL** 0 mg, **SODIUM** 212 mg, **CARB** 9 g (5 g fiber, 4 g sugars), **PRO** 5 g

## Broccoli with Goat Cheese and Walnuts

**8g**
CARB

| | |
|---|---|
| **SERVES** 6 | |
| **TOTAL** 30 min. | |

- 1 lb. broccoli, trimmed and cut into 1-inch pieces
- ½ cup buttermilk
- 1 Tbsp. snipped fresh parsley
- 1 Tbsp. Dijon mustard
- 2 tsp. olive oil
- 1 tsp. snipped fresh thyme
- 1 tsp. red wine vinegar
- 1 clove garlic, minced
- ⅛ tsp. salt
- ⅛ tsp. ground nutmeg
- ⅛ tsp. black pepper
- ½ cup thinly sliced red onion
- ¼ cup coarsely chopped walnuts, toasted
- ¼ cup crumbled semisoft goat cheese (chèvre) or feta cheese

1. In a covered 4-qt. saucepan cook broccoli in a small amount of lightly salted boiling water 6 to 8 minutes or until crisp-tender. Drain.
2. In a large bowl whisk together the next 10 ingredients (through pepper). Add broccoli and red onion; stir gently to coat. Top with walnuts and goat cheese.

**PER SERVING** *(½ cup each)* **CAL** 104, **FAT** 7 g (2 g sat. fat), **CHOL** 5 mg, **SODIUM** 171 mg, **CARB** 8 g (3 g fiber, 3 g sugars), **PRO** 5 g

**To Make Ahead** Prepare as directed, except do not top with walnuts and goat cheese. Cover and chill up to 4 hours. To serve, top with walnuts and goat cheese.

**Broccoli with Goat Cheese and Walnuts**

Cauliflower
"Couscous"

## Cauliflower "Couscous"

**14 g**
**CARB**

**SERVES** 8
**TOTAL** 50 min.

- ¼ cup dried cranberries
- ¼ cup snipped dried apricots
- 2 medium heads cauliflower (1½ to 2 lb. each), cored and cut into florets (8 cups)
- 2 Tbsp. butter
- 1 Tbsp. olive oil
- 1 medium onion, halved and thinly sliced
- 2 cloves garlic, minced

- 1 5-oz. pkg. fresh baby spinach, chopped
- ½ cup toasted walnuts, chopped
- ½ tsp. salt
- ½ cup sliced green onions

**1.** Place the dried cranberries and apricots in a small bowl. Cover with boiling water and let stand about 10 minutes or until plump; drain well.
**2.** Meanwhile, place the cauliflower, in batches, in a food processor. Cover and pulse until crumbly and mixture resembles the texture of couscous.

**3.** In a 12-inch skillet heat 1 Tbsp. of the butter and the olive oil over medium-high. Add the onion; cook and stir about 3 minutes or until tender and just starting to brown. Add garlic; cook and stir 30 seconds more. Add the cauliflower, spreading in an even layer. Cook about 8 minutes or until cauliflower is evenly golden, stirring occasionally. Spread in an even layer.
**4.** Add the drained cranberries and apricots, the spinach, walnuts, and salt. Cook and stir until combined. Stir in the remaining 1 Tbsp. butter and the green onions. Transfer to a bowl.

**PER SERVING** *(about 1 cup each)* **CAL** 139, **FAT** 8 g (3 g sat. fat), **CHOL** 8 mg, **SODIUM** 217 mg, **CARB** 14 g (4 g fiber, 7 g sugars), **PRO** 4 g

**To Make Ahead** Prepare as directed through Step 3. Place in an airtight container; cover. Chill up to 24 hours. To serve, reheat the cauliflower mixture in a lightly-oiled 12-inch skillet. Continue as directed. Or prepare the recipe as directed through Step 5. Cover and let stand at room temperature up to 4 hours. Serve at room temperature.

## Pan-Roasted Mushrooms

**7g**
**CARB**

**SERVES** 4
**TOTAL** 30 min.

- 12 oz. fresh mushrooms (such as cremini, stemmed shiitake, and/or button), halved
- ½ cup chopped red onion
- 1 Tbsp. olive oil
- 2 garlic, minced
- 2 Tbsp. balsamic vinegar
- 1 Tbsp. snipped fresh thyme
- ¼ tsp. salt
- ⅛ tsp. black pepper

**1.** In a 12-inch skillet cook mushrooms and onion in hot oil over medium 10 to 12 minutes or until tender and golden, stirring occasionally. Add garlic; cook and stir 30 seconds more. Remove from heat. Carefully add vinegar, thyme, salt, and pepper. Toss to coat.

**PER SERVING** *(½ cup each)* **CAL** 69, **FAT** 3 g (0 g sat. fat), **CHOL** 0 mg, **SODIUM** 153 mg, **CARB** 7 g (1 g fiber, 3 g sugars), **PRO** 2 g

**Pan-Roasted Mushrooms**

## Roasted Rosemary Delicata Squash

**16 g** CARB

**SERVES** 9
**HANDS ON** 10 min.
**TOTAL** 40 min.

- 2 1-lb. delicata squash, halved, seeded, and cut into ½-inch-thick slices
- 2 shallots, cut into wedges
- 2 Tbsp. olive oil
- 2 tsp. snipped fresh rosemary
- ½ tsp. salt
- ¼ tsp. black pepper
- ¼ cup finely shredded Parmesan cheese
  Chopped walnuts, toasted (optional)

**1.** Preheat oven to 425°F. Line a 15×10-inch baking pan with foil; lightly coat with *nonstick cooking spray*.
**2.** Place squash and shallots in a large bowl. Drizzle with olive oil and sprinkle with rosemary, salt, and pepper; toss to coat. Arrange squash mixture in a single layer in the prepared pan.
**3.** Roast about 30 minutes or until squash is tender and golden, turning once. Sprinkle with cheese and, if desired, walnuts.

**PER SERVING** *(½ cup each)* **CAL** 97, **FAT** 4 g (1 g sat. fat), **CHOL** 2 mg, **SODIUM** 172 mg, **CARB** 16 g (5 g fiber, 4 g sugars), **PRO** 2 g

Squash-Tomato Bake with Basil and Pine Nut Gremolata

Roasted Rosemary Delicata Squash

## Squash-Tomato Bake with Basil and Pine Nut Gremolata

**13 g** CARB

**SERVES** 6
**HANDS ON** 30 min.
**TOTAL** 1 hr. 30 min.

- 1 12-oz. jar roasted red sweet peppers, drained
- 1 8-oz. can no-salt-added tomato sauce
- 3 cloves garlic, halved

**QUICK TIP** For squash rounds, slice squash and then scoop seeds and stringy flesh out of each.

1½  tsp. dried Italian seasoning, crushed
⅛  to ¼ tsp. crushed red pepper (optional)
1½  lb. tomatoes, cored
1  1-lb. delicata squash, trimmed
1  large zucchini, trimmed
½  cup thinly sliced fresh basil
⅓  cup crumbled reduced-fat feta cheese
¼  cup pine nuts, toasted
1  tsp. lemon zest

**1.** Preheat oven to 375°F. For sauce, in a blender combine the first five ingredients (through crushed red pepper). Cover and blend until smooth. Spread sauce in a 2-qt. rectangular baking dish.
**2.** Cut tomatoes, squash, and zucchini into ¼-inch slices. Using a spoon, remove seeds from squash slices. Alternately arrange tomato, squash, and zucchini slices in two lengthwise rows over sauce in baking dish, standing slices slightly upright.

**3.** Bake, covered, 45 to 50 minutes or just until vegetables are tender. Cool slightly.
**4.** Meanwhile, for gremolata, in a bowl stir together the remaining ingredients. Sprinkle gremolata over vegetables.

**PER SERVING** (⅔ cup each) **CAL** 109, **FAT** 5 g (1 g sat. fat), **CHOL** 2 mg, **SODIUM** 206 mg, **CARB** 13 g (4 g fiber, 8 g sugars), **PRO** 5 g

# Maple-Thyme Roasted Baby Carrots

**26 g** **CARB**

| | |
|---|---|
| **SERVES** 8 | |
| **HANDS ON** 25 min. | |
| **TOTAL** 50 min. | |

- 5 lb. baby carrots with tops, peeled and tops trimmed
- 3 Tbsp. olive oil
- 1 tsp. freshly ground black pepper
- ½ tsp. kosher salt
- ¼ cup maple syrup
- 8 cloves garlic, minced
- 1 Tbsp. butter, melted
- 2 Tbsp. snipped fresh thyme

**1.** Place two 15×10-inch baking pans in oven. Preheat oven to 450°F.

**2.** Halve any large carrots lengthwise. In a large bowl combine carrots, oil, pepper, and salt; toss to coat. Carefully spread carrots in heated pans.

**3.** Roast 20 to 25 minutes or until carrots are tender and starting to brown, rearranging pans and stirring carrots halfway through roasting. Drizzle with maple syrup and sprinkle with garlic; toss to coat. Roast about 5 minutes more or until carrots are glazed and syrup is bubbly. Drizzle with melted butter and sprinkle with thyme.

**4.** Reserve 8 oz. roasted carrots (1½ cups cut up) for Arugula Salad with Carrots and Goat Cheese (p. 109). Serve the remaining carrots immediately.

**PER SERVING** (4 oz. each) **CAL** 154, **FAT** 6 g (1 g sat. fat), **CHOL** 3 mg, **SODIUM** 206 mg, **CARB** 26 g (6 g fiber, 14 g sugars), **PRO** 2 g

**Tip** If you can't find baby carrots, use regular or heirloom multicolor carrots, halved lengthwise.

**Maple-Thyme Roasted Baby Carrots**

**Sweet Potato and Wild Rice Dressing**

**Brussels Sprouts with Bacon and Cider Vinegar** *recipe, p. 102*

## Sweet Potato and Wild Rice Dressing

**30 g CARB**

| | |
|---|---|
| **SERVES** 8 |
| **HANDS ON** 20 min. |
| **TOTAL** 1 hr. |

- 2½ cups water
- ½ cup regular pearled barley
- ½ cup uncooked wild rice, rinsed and drained
- 2 lb. sweet potatoes, peeled and cut into ¾-inch pieces
- 3 Tbsp. olive oil
- 6 cloves garlic, minced
- 1 tsp. kosher salt
- 1 tsp. black pepper
- ¼ cup snipped fresh parsley
- ¼ cup chopped green onions
- 1 tsp. snipped fresh rosemary
- ⅓ cup pomegranate seeds

**1.** In a 2-qt. saucepan combine the water and barley. Bring to boiling. Stir in wild rice; reduce heat. Simmer, covered, about 40 minutes or until tender. Drain off any excess water.

**2.** Meanwhile, place a 15×10-inch baking pan in oven. Preheat oven to 450°F.

**3.** In a large bowl combine sweet potatoes, 2 Tbsp. of the oil, the garlic, and ½ tsp. each of the salt and pepper. Carefully spread potatoes in heated pan. Roast about 25 minutes or until tender and browned, stirring once after 10 minutes. Reserve 1½ cups roasted sweet potatoes for Sweet Potato, Sausage, and Goat Cheese Egg Casserole *(p. 9)*.

**4.** In a serving dish combine wild rice mixture and the remaining sweet potatoes, 1 Tbsp. oil, and ½ tsp. each salt and pepper. Add parsley, green onions, and rosemary; toss to combine. Sprinkle with pomegranate seeds.

**PER SERVING** *(⅔ cup each)* **CAL** 169, **FAT** 4 g (1 g sat. fat), **CHOL** 0 mg, **SODIUM** 148 mg, **CARB** 30 g (5 g fiber, 4 g sugars), **PRO** 4 g

## Brussels Sprouts with Bacon and Cider Vinegar

**16 g**
**CARB**

**SERVES** 8
**HANDS ON** 30 min.
**TOTAL** 40 min.

- 2 lb. Brussels sprouts, trimmed and halved
- 1 cup water
- ½ tsp. kosher salt
- 4 slices center-cut bacon, chopped
- 3 Tbsp. olive oil
- 2 Tbsp. finely chopped shallot
- 4 cloves garlic, minced
- ¼ cup cider vinegar
- 2 Tbsp. honey
- 2 tsp. whole grain mustard
- ½ tsp. black pepper

**1.** In a 12-inch skillet combine Brussels sprouts, the water, and ¼ tsp. of the salt. Bring to boiling; reduce heat. Simmer, covered, 5 to 7 minutes or until tender. Drain in a colander.

**2.** In same skillet cook bacon over medium 5 to 6 minutes or until crisp. Drain bacon on paper towels; drain fat from skillet.

**3.** Add oil, shallot, and garlic to skillet; cook 3 to 4 minutes or until shallot is tender. Whisk in vinegar, 1 Tbsp. of the honey, the mustard, pepper, and the remaining ¼ tsp. salt. Cook, uncovered, 6 to 8 minutes or until slightly thick. Stir in sprouts; heat through.

**4.** Sprinkle Brussels sprout mixture with bacon and drizzle with the remaining 1 Tbsp. honey.

**PER SERVING** (¾ cup each) **CAL** 130, **FAT** 6 g (1 g sat. fat), **CHOL** 4 mg, **SODIUM** 168 mg, **CARB** 16 g (4 g fiber, 7 g sugars), **PRO** 6 g

## Pan-Roasted Veggies

**9 g**
**CARB**

**SERVES** 4
**TOTAL** 25 min.

- 1 Tbsp. sugar*
- 1 Tbsp. water
- 1 Tbsp. reduced-sodium soy sauce
- 2 tsp. cider vinegar
- 1 to 2 tsp. sriracha sauce
- 2 tsp. canola oil
- 1 8-oz. pkg. whole fresh button mushrooms
- 8 miniature sweet peppers
- ½ cup grape tomatoes

**1.** For sauce, in a bowl stir together the first five ingredients (through sriracha sauce).

**2.** Heat a 10-inch cast-iron skillet over medium about 5 minutes or until very hot. Add oil to skillet. Add mushrooms and sweet peppers; cook 8 to 10 minutes or until vegetables begin to char, stirring once or twice. Add sauce; cook until slightly reduced. Add tomatoes; cook 1 minute more, stirring to coat vegetables with sauce. Serve immediately or at room temperature.

**PER SERVING** (¾ cup each) **CAL** 64, **FAT** 3 g (0 g sat. fat), **CHOL** 0 mg, **SODIUM** 173 mg, **CARB** 9 g (2 g fiber, 7 g sugars), **PRO** 3 g

**\*Sugar Sub** We do not recommend a sugar sub for this recipe.

## Roasted Radishes with Orange Vinaigrette

**5 g**
**CARB**

**SERVES** 6
**HANDS ON** 15 min.
**TOTAL** 45 min.

1½ lb. radishes, trimmed and halved
3 Tbsp. olive oil
1 orange
1 Tbsp. sherry vinegar or white wine vinegar
1 tsp. honey
¼ tsp. salt
¼ tsp. black pepper

**1.** Preheat oven to 425°F. Place radishes in a 15×10-inch baking pan. Drizzle with 1 Tbsp. of the oil; toss to coat. Roast 30 to 35 minutes or until tender and lightly browned, stirring once.

**2.** Meanwhile, remove ½ tsp. zest and squeeze 1 Tbsp. juice from orange. For vinaigrette, in a small screw-top jar combine remaining ingredients and the remaining 2 Tbsp. oil. Cover and shake well. Drizzle vinaigrette over radishes.

PER SERVING *(½ cup each)* **CAL** 83, **FAT** 7 g (1 g sat. fat), **CHOL** 0 mg, **SODIUM** 141 mg, **CARB** 5 g (2 g fiber, 3 g sugars), **PRO** 1 g

**Roasted Radishes with Orange Vinaigrette**

## Honey-Butter Turnips

**16 g**
**CARB**

**SERVES** 5
**HANDS ON** 15 min.
**TOTAL** 50 min.

1 to 1½ lb. turnips, peeled and cut into 1¼-inch pieces
3 Tbsp. honey
2 Tbsp. unsalted butter, melted
¼ tsp. salt

⅛ **tsp. cracked black pepper**
**Snipped fresh thyme**

**1.** Preheat oven to 400°F. Heat a
15×10-inch baking pan in oven
5 minutes. Carefully spread turnips in
heated pan. Drizzle with honey and
melted butter and sprinkle with salt.
**2.** Roast 35 to 40 minutes or until
turnips are tender, stirring once.

Transfer to a serving dish. Sprinkle
with pepper and thyme. If desired,
drizzle with additional honey.

**PER SERVING** *(½ cup each)* **CAL** 105,
**FAT** 5 g (3 g sat. fat), **CHOL** 12 mg,
**SODIUM** 178 mg, **CARB** 16 g (2 g fiber,
14 g sugars), **PRO** 1 g

**QUICK TIP** Beets bleed their bright magenta color and can stain your hands and anything they come in contact with. Wear plastic gloves when working with them.

## Beet, Fennel, and Apple Slaw

**17 g**
**CARB**

| **SERVES** 8 |
| **TOTAL** 25 min. |

3  Tbsp. olive oil
3  Tbsp. white balsamic vinegar, white wine vinegar, or cider vinegar
3  Tbsp. orange juice
2  cloves garlic, minced
¼  tsp. salt
2  oranges, peeled and cut into segments
1  medium red beet, trimmed, halved lengthwise, cored, and cut into matchsticks
1  medium apple, cored and sliced
1  fennel bulb, trimmed, halved lengthwise, cored, and cut into matchsticks
1  small jicama, peeled and cut into matchsticks
½  cup firmly packed chopped fresh Italian parsley

**1.** For vinaigrette, in a screw-top jar combine the first five ingredients (through salt). Cover and shake well. For slaw, in a bowl toss together the remaining ingredients. Add vinaigrette; gently toss to coat.

**PER SERVING** (⅓ to ½ cup each) **CAL** 114, **FAT** 5 g (1 g sat. fat), **CHOL** 0 mg, **SODIUM** 100 mg, **CARB** 17 g (4 g fiber, 10 g sugars), **PRO** 1 g

**To Make Ahead** Prepare vinaigrette as directed. Store in the refrigerator up to 1 week. Let stand at room temperature before serving. Or finished slaw can be covered and stored in the refrigerator up to 4 hours. If refrigerated, let stand at room temperature 30 minutes before serving.

Fresh Asparagus-
Tomato Salad

## Fresh Asparagus-Tomato Salad

**7g** CARB | **SERVES** 4
**TOTAL** 20 min.

- 2 cups mixed salad greens or baby spinach
- 1 lb. thin fresh asparagus, trimmed and cut diagonally into 1½-inch pieces
- 1 cup cherry tomatoes, halved
- ½ cup fresh basil leaves, large leaves torn
- 2 Tbsp. white wine vinegar
- 4 tsp. olive oil
- 1 tsp. honey
- ⅛ tsp. salt
- ⅛ tsp. black pepper
- 2 Tbsp. finely shredded Parmesan cheese
- 2 Tbsp. pine nuts or chopped walnuts, toasted

**1.** In a large bowl combine salad greens, asparagus, tomatoes, and basil.
**2.** For vinaigrette, in a small screw-top jar combine vinegar, oil, honey, salt, and pepper. Cover and shake well.
**3.** Pour vinaigrette over greens mixture; toss gently to coat. Sprinkle with cheese and nuts.

PER SERVING (1¼ cups each) **CAL** 112, **FAT** 8 g (1 g sat. fat), **CHOL** 2 mg, **SODIUM** 123 mg, **CARB** 7 g (2 g fiber, 4 g sugars), **PRO** 4 g

## Arugula Salad with Carrots and Goat Cheese

**11g** CARB | **SERVES** 8
**TOTAL** 20 min.

- 3 Tbsp. olive oil
- 2 Tbsp. finely chopped shallot
- 1½ Tbsp. sherry vinegar or cider vinegar
- 1 Tbsp. pure maple syrup
- 1½ tsp. lemon juice
- 1 tsp. snipped fresh thyme
- 1 tsp. Dijon mustard
- ½ tsp. black pepper
- ¼ tsp. kosher salt
- 1 5-oz. pkg. baby arugula
- 1½ cups cut-up roasted carrots (from Maple-Thyme Roasted Baby Carrots, p. 100)
- 2 Tbsp. chopped walnuts, toasted
- ¼ cup pomegranate seeds
- 2 Tbsp. crumbled goat (chèvre), feta, or blue cheese or shaved Parmesan cheese

**1.** For vinaigrette, in a small bowl whisk together the first nine ingredients (through salt).
**2.** In a large bowl combine arugula, carrots, and walnuts. Drizzle with vinaigrette; toss to coat. Sprinkle with pomegranate seeds and cheese.

PER SERVING (¾ cup each) **CAL** 120, **FAT** 8 g (2 g sat. fat), **CHOL** 2 mg, **SODIUM** 114 mg, **CARB** 11 g (2 g fiber, 6 g sugars), **PRO** 2 g

**Tip** Look for sherry vinegar in the specialty oil and vinegar section in the grocery store.

Arugula Salad with Carrots and Goat Cheese

Kale Salad
with Dates

## Kale Salad with Dates

**10 g** **SERVES** 24
CARB **TOTAL** 35 min.

1½ lb. rinsed and drained kale, stemmed and chopped (about 15 cups)
5 Tbsp. lemon juice
1¼ tsp. kosher salt
¼ cup olive oil
1 shallot, minced
2 Tbsp. honey
½ tsp. crushed red pepper

1 cup pecan halves, toasted and chopped
1 large Honeycrisp apple, quartered, cored, and sliced
3 oz. Pecorino Romano cheese, shaved
½ cup pitted dates, chopped (about 10 dates)

**1.** Place chopped kale in a large salad bowl. Drizzle 3 Tbsp. of the lemon juice and sprinkle ¼ tsp. of the salt over the kale. Using clean hands, massage the leaves gently 4 to 5 minutes or until tender and glossy.

**2.** For dressing, in a small screw-top jar combine olive oil, shallot, honey, the remaining 2 Tbsp. lemon juice and 1 tsp. salt, and the crushed red pepper. Cover and shake well.

**3.** Add pecans, apple, cheese, and dates to kale. Add dressing; toss.

PER SERVING (½ cup each) **CAL** 105, **FAT** 7 g (1 g sat. fat), **CHOL** 4 mg, **SODIUM** 125 mg, **CARB** 10 g (2 g fiber, 6 g sugars), **PRO** 3 g

## Snap Pea Salad with Lemon and Feta

**9 g**
**CARB**

**SERVES** 4
**TOTAL** 25 min.

4 tsp. olive oil
1 Tbsp. Meyer lemon juice
½ tsp. Dijon mustard
⅛ tsp. kosher salt
⅛ tsp. black pepper
½ of a medium fennel bulb, leafy fronds reserved
2 cups sugar snap pea pods, trimmed and halved diagonally
1 cup baby arugula
4 radishes, thinly sliced
½ cup crumbled feta cheese (2 oz.)
1 Meyer lemon, thinly sliced

**1.** For dressing, in a small bowl whisk together oil, lemon juice, mustard, salt, and pepper.
**2.** Trim, halve, core, and thinly slice fennel bulb. In a large bowl combine sliced fennel, snap peas, arugula, and radishes. Drizzle with dressing; toss to coat.
**3.** Top servings with cheese and fennel fronds. Serve with lemon slices.

**PER SERVING** *(1 cup each)* **CAL** 108, **FAT** 8 g (3 g sat. fat), **CHOL** 13 mg, **SODIUM** 200 mg, **CARB** 9 g (3 g fiber, 4 g sugars), **PRO** 4 g

Snap Pea Salad with Lemon and Feta

# 6

# FRESH-BAKED
# BREADS

Nothing is better than the smell of fresh-baked bread, something

you can enjoy on special occasions. Include this variety of options

in your holiday meal plans—each recipe is light on carbs and

right-portioned for you. Serve these loaves, muffins, and rolls on a

brunch buffet or alongside soups and festive dinners.

## Chocolate-Swirled Pumpkin Bread

**21 g**
CARB

| | |
|---|---|
| **SERVES** | 16 |
| **HANDS ON** | 25 min. |
| **TOTAL** | 2 hr. 15 min. |

Nonstick cooking spray
3 oz. bittersweet chocolate, chopped
3 Tbsp. water
2 Tbsp. packed brown sugar*
2 Tbsp. chopped pecans
2 tsp. chilled butter
1¾ cups all-purpose flour
1 tsp. baking soda
1 tsp. pumpkin pie spice
½ tsp. salt
2 eggs, lightly beaten
¾ cup canned pumpkin
⅓ cup maple syrup
¼ cup unsweetened applesauce
¼ cup canola oil
1 tsp. vanilla

**1.** Preheat oven to 350°F. Coat a 9×5-inch loaf pan with cooking spray. In a small saucepan cook and stir chocolate and the water over low until melted and smooth; cool.
**2.** Meanwhile, in a small bowl stir together brown sugar and pecans. Using a fork, cut in butter until crumbly.
**3.** In a large bowl combine flour, baking soda, pumpkin pie spice, and salt. In a medium bowl combine the remaining ingredients. Add pumpkin mixture to flour mixture; stir just until moistened.
**4.** Spread half of the batter into the prepared loaf pan. Drizzle with half of the melted chocolate. Using a narrow metal spatula, swirl chocolate into batter. Repeat with the remaining batter and chocolate. Sprinkle with pecan mixture.
**5.** Bake 40 to 45 minutes or until a toothpick comes out clean. Cool in pan on a wire rack 10 minutes. Remove; cool completely on wire rack.

**PER SERVING** (1 slice each) **CAL** 156, **FAT** 7 g (2 g sat. fat), **CHOL** 25 mg, **SODIUM** 166 mg, **CARB** 21 g (1 g fiber, 9 g sugars), **PRO** 3 g

*Sugar Sub We do not recommend a sugar sub for this recipe.

## Refrigerator Whole Wheat Pumpkin Muffins

**17 g**
CARB

| | |
|---|---|
| **SERVES** | 24 |
| **HANDS ON** | 15 min. |
| **TOTAL** | 35 min. |

1½ cups whole wheat flour
1 cup all-purpose flour
½ cup packed brown sugar*
½ cup chopped walnuts, toasted
4 tsp. baking powder
1 Tbsp. pumpkin pie spice
¾ tsp. baking soda
½ tsp. salt
1 15-oz. can pumpkin
1½ cups buttermilk
½ cup refrigerated or frozen egg product, thawed
¼ cup butter, melted
2 tsp. lemon zest
Nonstick cooking spray

**1.** In a large bowl stir together the first eight ingredients (through salt). Make a well in the center of the flour mixture. In another bowl combine the next five ingredients (through lemon zest). Add egg mixture all at once to flour mixture. Stir just until moistened. Place plastic wrap over the surface of the batter.

Cover tightly; refrigerate up to 3 days (or bake immediately).
**2.** To bake, preheat oven to 400°F. Coat as many 2½-inch muffin cups as needed to bake desired number of muffins with cooking spray. Spoon about ¼ cup of the batter into each prepared muffin cup.
**3.** Bake 15 to 18 minutes or until toothpick comes out clean. Cool in muffin cups on a wire rack 5 minutes. Remove; cool completely on rack.

**PER SERVING** (1 muffin each) **CAL** 113, **FAT** 4 g (2 g sat. fat), **CHOL** 6 mg, **SODIUM** 215 mg, **CARB** 17 g (2 g fiber, 6 g sugars), **PRO** 3 g

*Sugar Sub Choose Splenda Brown Sugar Blend. Follow package directions to use ½ cup equivalent.

**PER SERVING WITH SUB** Same as above, except **CAL** 106, **SODIUM** 213, **CARB** 14 g (4 g sugars)

Tip To toast whole nuts or large pieces, spread in a shallow baking pan lined with parchment paper. Bake in a 350°F oven 5 to 10 minutes or until golden, shaking pan once or twice.

**Refrigerator Whole Wheat Pumpkin Muffins**

Berry Morning Muffins

## Berry Morning Muffins

**23 g CARB**

| | |
|---|---|
| **SERVES** 12 | |
| **HANDS ON** 15 min. | |
| **TOTAL** 35 min. | |

Nonstick cooking spray
1½ cups whole wheat flour
2 tsp. ground cinnamon
1 tsp. baking powder
1 tsp. baking soda
¼ tsp. ground nutmeg
2 eggs, lightly beaten
¾ cup unsweetened applesauce

¼ cup agave syrup
1½ tsp. vanilla
1 cup fresh raspberries and/or halved strawberries
3 oz. 70% to 80% dark chocolate, chopped
⅓ cup chopped walnuts

**1.** Preheat oven to 350°F. Coat twelve 2½-inch muffin cups with cooking spray. In a large bowl stir together the next five ingredients (through nutmeg). Make a well in center of flour mixture.

**2.** In a small bowl combine eggs, applesauce, agave syrup, and vanilla. Add egg mixture all at once to flour mixture. Stir just until moistened. Fold in berries, chocolate, and walnuts. Spoon batter into the prepared muffin cups, filling each three-fourths full.
**3.** Bake 18 to 20 minutes or until a toothpick comes out clean. Cool in muffin cups on a wire rack.

**PER SERVING** (1 muffin each) **CAL** 162, **FAT** 6 g (2 g sat. fat), **CHOL** 31 mg, **SODIUM** 160 mg, **CARB** 23 g (3 g fiber, 9 g sugars), **PRO** 4 g

## Lemon Bread

**22g** CARB | **SERVES** 16
**HANDS ON** 20 min.
**TOTAL** 1 hr. 20 min.

- 1¾ cups all-purpose flour
- ¾ cup sugar*
- 2 tsp. baking powder
- ¼ tsp. salt
- 1 lemon
- 1 egg, lightly beaten
- 1 cup milk
- ¼ cup vegetable oil or butter, melted
- ½ cup chopped walnuts or almonds
- 2 Tbsp. lemon juice (optional)
- 1 Tbsp. sugar* (optional)

**1.** Preheat oven to 350°F. Grease the bottom and ½ inch up the sides of an 8×4-inch loaf pan. In a medium bowl stir together flour, the ¾ cup sugar, the baking powder, and salt. Make a well in center of flour mixture.
**2.** Remove 2 tsp. zest and squeeze 3 Tbsp. juice from lemon (2 Tbsp. is optional). In another medium bowl combine egg, milk, oil, lemon zest, and 1 Tbsp. of the lemon juice. Add egg mixture all at once to flour mixture. Stir just until moistened (batter should be lumpy). Stir in nuts. Spoon batter into the prepared pan, spreading evenly.
**3.** Bake 50 to 55 minutes or until a toothpick comes out clean. If desired, in a small bowl stir together the remaining 2 Tbsp. lemon juice and the 1 Tbsp. sugar; brush over top of hot loaf. Cool in pan on a wire rack 10 minutes. Remove; cool completely on wire rack. Wrap and store overnight before slicing.

**Lemon-Poppy Seed Bread** Prepare as directed, except substitute 1 Tbsp. poppy seeds for the almonds or walnuts.

**PER SERVING** (1 slice each) **CAL** 153, **FAT** 7 g (1 g sat. fat), **CHOL** 13 mg, **SODIUM** 109 mg, **CARB** 22 g (1 g fiber, 10 g sugars), **PRO** 3 g

*****Sugar Sub** Choose Splenda Sugar Blend. Follow package directions to use ¾ cup equivalent for bread. We do not recommend a sugar sub for the optional glaze.

**PER SERVING WITH SUB** Same as original, except **CAL** 139, **CARB** 16 g (5 g sugars)

Lemon Bread

## BANANA BREAD 5 WAYS

Basic banana bread can be your building block for an array of flavors. Pick your favorite or make one of each as sweet gifts or breakfast treats.

*recipes, pp. 120 and 121*

*pictured on pp. 118 and 119*

## Sweet Potato Banana Bread

**20 g** CARB

**SERVES** 16
**HANDS ON** 20 min.
**TOTAL** 1 hr. 20 min.

Nonstick cooking spray
1½ cups all-purpose flour
1 tsp. baking soda
1 tsp. ground cinnamon
¼ tsp. salt
⅛ tsp. ground cloves
1 cup shredded sweet potato (4 oz.)
⅔ cup mashed ripe bananas (about 2 medium)
1 6-oz. carton plain fat-free Greek yogurt
½ cup packed brown sugar*
½ cup refrigerated or frozen egg product, thawed
⅓ cup canola oil
¼ cup chopped pecans, toasted

**1.** Preheat oven to 350°F. Coat bottom and sides of a 9×5-inch loaf pan with cooking spray. In a large bowl combine flour, baking soda, cinnamon, salt, and cloves. Make a well in center of flour mixture.
**2.** In a medium bowl stir together the next six ingredients (through oil). Add egg mixture all at once to flour mixture; stir until evenly moistened. Fold in pecans. Spoon batter into prepared pan.
**3.** Bake 50 to 55 minutes or until a toothpick comes out clean. If necessary to prevent overbrowning, cover loosely with foil the last 15 minutes of baking. Cool in pan on a wire rack 10 minutes. Remove from pan; cool completely on wire rack. Wrap in plastic wrap or foil; store overnight before slicing.

**PER SERVING** *(1 slice each)* **CAL** 143, **FAT** 6 g (0 g sat. fat), **CHOL** 0 mg, **SODIUM** 140 mg, **CARB** 20 g (1 g fiber, 8 g sugars), **PRO** 3 g

***Sugar Sub** We do not recommend a sugar sub for this recipe.

## Cocoa Hazelnut Banana Bread

**23 g** CARB

**SERVES** 16
**HANDS ON** 20 min.
**TOTAL** 1 hr. 15 min.

Nonstick cooking spray
1¾ cups all-purpose flour
2 Tbsp. unsweetened cocoa powder
1 tsp. baking soda
¼ tsp. salt
2 eggs, lightly beaten
1 cup mashed ripe bananas (about 3 medium)
1 6-oz. carton plain fat-free Greek yogurt
½ cup packed brown sugar*
¼ cup chocolate-hazelnut spread, such as Nutella
2 Tbsp. canola oil
¼ cup chopped hazelnuts

**1.** Preheat oven to 350°F. Coat one 9×5-inch loaf pan or two 7×3½-inch loaf pans with cooking spray; if desired, line bottom with parchment paper. In a large bowl combine flour, cocoa powder, baking soda, and salt. Make a well in center of flour mixture.
**2.** In a medium bowl stir together the next six ingredients (through oil). Add banana mixture all at once to flour mixture; stir until evenly moistened. Spoon batter into prepared pan(s). Sprinkle top(s) evenly with hazelnuts.
**3.** Bake 45 to 50 minutes for the 9×5-inch pan or 30 to 35 minutes for the 7×3½-inch pans or until a toothpick comes out clean. If necessary to prevent overbrowning, cover loosely with foil the last 15 minutes of baking. Cool in pan(s) on wire rack(s) 10 minutes. Remove from pan(s); cool completely on wire rack(s). Peel off parchment paper if using. Wrap in plastic wrap or foil; store overnight before slicing.

**PER SERVING** *(1 slice each)* **CAL** 152, **FAT** 5 g (1 g sat. fat), **CHOL** 23 mg, **SODIUM** 132 mg, **CARB** 23 g (1 g fiber, 11 g sugars), **PRO** 4 g

***Sugar Sub** Choose Splenda Brown Sugar Blend. Follow package directions to use ½ cup brown sugar equivalent.

**PER SERVING WITH SUB** Same as original, except **CAL** 141, **CARB** 20 g (7g sugars)

## Almond Cranberry Banana Bread

**23 g** CARB

**SERVES** 16
**HANDS ON** 20 min.
**TOTAL** 1 hr. 15 min.

Nonstick cooking spray
1½ cups all-purpose flour
½ cup whole wheat flour
½ cup dried cranberries
⅓ cup sliced almonds
1½ tsp. baking powder
1 tsp. ground cinnamon
½ tsp. baking soda
¼ tsp. salt
⅔ cup mashed ripe bananas (about 2 medium)
½ cup refrigerated or frozen egg product, thawed, or 2 eggs, lightly beaten
⅓ cup honey
⅓ cup orange juice
¼ cup butter, melted
¼ tsp. almond extract

**1.** Preheat oven to 350°F. Coat the bottom and sides of a 9×5-inch loaf pan with cooking spray or line with parchment paper. In a large bowl combine the next eight ingredients (through salt). Make a well in center of flour mixture.
**2.** In a medium bowl combine the next six ingredients (through almond extract). Add egg mixture all at once to flour mixture; stir until evenly moistened. Spoon batter into prepared pan.
**3.** Bake about 45 minutes or until a toothpick comes out clean. If necessary to prevent overbrowning, cover loosely with foil the last 15 minutes of baking. Cool in pan on a

wire rack 10 minutes. Remove from pan; cool completely on wire rack. Wrap in plastic wrap or foil; store overnight before slicing.

PER SERVING (1 slice each) **CAL** 138, **FAT** 4 g (2 g sat. fat), **CHOL** 8 mg, **SODIUM** 162 mg, **CARB** 23 g (1 g fiber, 10 g sugars), **PRO** 3 g

## Pineapple Coconut Banana Bread

**19 g**
CARB

**SERVES** 16
**HANDS ON** 20 min.
**TOTAL** 1 hr. 25 min.

Nonstick cooking spray
1 cup all-purpose flour
1 cup whole wheat flour
¼ cup flaked coconut, toasted
1 tsp. baking soda
1 tsp. ground ginger
¼ tsp. salt
⅔ cup mashed ripe bananas (about 2 medium)
1 6-oz. carton plain fat-free Greek yogurt
½ cup refrigerated or frozen egg product, thawed
⅓ cup packed brown sugar*
¼ cup canned crushed pineapple (juice pack), well drained
¼ cup butter, melted
1 tsp. vanilla

**1.** Preheat oven to 350°F. Coat bottom and sides of a 9×5-inch loaf pan with cooking spray or line with parchment paper. In a large bowl combine the next six ingredients (through salt). Make a well in center of flour mixture.
**2.** In a medium bowl combine the next seven ingredients (through vanilla). Add egg mixture all at once to flour mixture; stir until evenly moistened. Spoon batter into prepared pan.
**3.** Bake 55 to 60 minutes or until a toothpick comes out clean. If necessary to prevent overbrowning, cover loosely with foil the last 15 minutes of baking. Cool in pan on a wire rack 10 minutes. Remove from

pan; cool completely on wire rack. Wrap in plastic wrap or foil; store overnight before slicing.

PER SERVING (1 slice each) **CAL** 120, **FAT** 4 g (2 g sat. fat), **CHOL** 8 mg, **SODIUM** 164 mg, **CARB** 19 g (1 g fiber, 7 g sugars), **PRO** 4 g

**\*Sugar Sub** Choose Splenda Brown Sugar Blend. Follow package directions to use ⅓ cup equivalent.

PER SERVING WITH SUB Same as above, except **CAL** 113, **CARB** 16 g (4 g sugars)

## Cheesecake Chai-Spiced Banana Bread

**18 g**
CARB

**SERVES** 16
**HANDS ON** 30 min.
**TOTAL** 1 hr. 30 min.

Nonstick cooking spray
1½ cups all-purpose flour
¼ cup regular rolled oats
1½ tsp. baking powder
¾ tsp. ground cardamom
¾ tsp. ground cinnamon
½ tsp. baking soda
¼ tsp. salt
¼ tsp. ground cloves
¼ tsp. ground allspice
4 egg whites
⅔ cup mashed ripe bananas (about 2 medium)
⅓ cup canola oil
¼ cup honey
¼ cup fat-free milk
4 oz. reduced-fat cream cheese (neufchatel), softened
2 Tbsp. all-purpose flour
1 Tbsp. honey
1 tsp. vanilla

**1.** Preheat oven to 350°F. Lightly coat a 9×5-inch loaf pan with cooking spray. If desired, line bottom of pan with parchment paper. In a large bowl stir together the next nine ingredients (through allspice). Make a well in the center of the flour mixture.

**2.** In a medium bowl combine two of the egg whites, the bananas, oil, the ¼ cup honey, and the milk.
**3.** In another medium bowl combine cream cheese, the remaining two egg whites, the 2 Tbsp. flour, the 1 Tbsp. honey, and the vanilla. Beat with a mixer on medium just until combined.
**4.** Add banana mixture all at once to flour mixture; stir until evenly moistened. Spoon two-thirds of batter into prepared baking pan. Spoon cream cheese mixture over batter in baking pan; spoon the remaining batter over all. Using a thin metal spatula or a table knife, cut down through the batter and pull up in a circular motion to marble the cream cheese layer.
**5.** Bake 50 to 60 minutes or until a toothpick comes out clean. If necessary to prevent overbrowning, cover loosely with foil the last 15 minutes of baking. Cool in pan on a wire rack 10 minutes. Remove from pan; cool completely on wire rack. Wrap in plastic wrap or foil; chill in the refrigerator overnight before slicing.

PER SERVING (1 slice each) **CAL** 142, **FAT** 7 g (1 g sat. fat), **CHOL** 5 mg, **SODIUM** 161 mg, **CARB** 18 g (1 g fiber, 7 g sugars), **PRO** 3 g

**Honey-Zucchini Bread**

## Honey-Zucchini Bread

**28 g**
**CARB**

| | |
|---|---|
| **SERVES** | 28 |
| **HANDS ON** | 25 min. |
| **TOTAL** | 1 hr. 35 min. |

 3 cups all-purpose flour
 1 Tbsp. baking powder
 1½ tsp. ground cinnamon
 1 tsp. salt
 2 eggs, lightly beaten
 2½ cups coarsely shredded unpeeled zucchini
 1½ cups sugar*
 1 cup vegetable oil
 ½ cup honey
 2 tsp. vanilla
 1 cup chopped walnuts or pecans (optional)
 ⅔ cup raisins (optional)
 ½ cup granola
 Honey (optional)

**1.** Preheat oven to 325°F. Grease the bottom and ½ inch up the sides of two 8×4-inch loaf pans. In a large bowl stir together flour, baking powder, cinnamon, and salt. Make a well in center of flour mixture.

**2.** In a medium bowl combine the next six ingredients (through vanilla). Add zucchini mixture all at once to flour mixture. Stir just until moistened (batter should be lumpy). If desired, stir in nuts and raisins. Spoon batter into the prepared loaf pans, spreading evenly. Sprinkle with granola.

**3.** Bake 60 to 70 minutes or until a toothpick comes out clean. If necessary to prevent overbrowning, cover loosely with foil the last 15 minutes of baking.

**4.** Cool in pans on wire racks 10 minutes. Remove from pans. Cool completely on wire racks. Wrap and store overnight before slicing. If desired, serve with additional honey.

**PER SERVING** (1 slice each) **CAL** 192, **FAT** 8 g (1 g sat. fat), **CHOL** 13 mg, **SODIUM** 146 mg, **CARB** 28 g (1 g fiber, 17 g sugars), **PRO** 2 g

*****Sugar Sub** Choose Splenda Sugar Blend. Follow package directions to use 1½ cups equivalent.

**PER SERVING WITH SUB** Same as above, except **CAL** 176, **CARB** 22 g (11 g sugars)

## Chive Batter Rolls

**23 g**
**CARB**

| | |
|---|---|
| **SERVES** | 12 |
| **HANDS ON** | 30 min. |
| **TOTAL** | 1 hr. 10 min. |

 1 Tbsp. yellow cornmeal
 2 cups all-purpose flour
 1 pkg. fast-rising active dry yeast
 ¼ tsp. black pepper
 1 cup milk
 3 Tbsp. butter
 2 Tbsp. sugar*
 ½ tsp. salt
 1 egg
 ½ cup snipped fresh chives or ¼ cup finely chopped green onions (green tops only)
 ⅓ cup yellow cornmeal

**1.** Grease the bottom and sides of twelve 2½-inch muffin cups. Sprinkle bottoms with 1 Tbsp. cornmeal. In a large mixing bowl stir together 1¼ cups of the flour, the yeast, and the pepper.

**2.** In a small saucepan combine milk, butter, sugar, and salt; heat and stir over medium just until mixture is warm (120°F to 130°F) and butter almost melts. Add milk mixture and egg to flour mixture. Beat with a mixer on low to medium 30 seconds, scraping bowl constantly. Beat on high 3 minutes. Stir in the chives and ⅓ cup cornmeal. Stir in remaining flour. (The batter will be soft and sticky.) Cover and let rest in a warm place 10 minutes.

**3.** Preheat oven to 350°F. Spoon batter into the prepared muffin cups. Cover loosely with plastic wrap. Let rise in a warm place 20 minutes.

**4.** Bake about 18 minutes or until rolls sound hollow when tapped. Cool in muffin cups 5 minutes. Loosen edges and remove. Serve warm.

**PER SERVING** (1 roll each) **CAL** 145, **FAT** 4 g (2 g sat. fat), **CHOL** 25 mg, **SODIUM** 136 mg, **CARB** 23 g (1 g fiber, 3 g sugars), **PRO** 4 g

*****Sugar Sub** Choose Splenda Sugar Blend. Follow package directions to use 2 Tbsp. equivalent.

**PER SERVING WITH SUB** Same as above, except **CAL** 142, **CARB** 22 g (2 g sugars)

Chive Batter Rolls

## Everyday Artisan Bread

**19 g CARB**

**SERVES** 30
**HANDS ON** 15 min.
**TOTAL** 3 hr.

6 cups all-purpose flour
1 cup Add-In (optional)
4 tsp. kosher salt
1 package active dry yeast
3 cups warm water (120°F to 130°F)
Cornmeal

1. In an extra-large bowl combine flour, Add-In (if desired), salt, and yeast. Stir in the warm water until mixture is moistened (dough will be very sticky and soft). Cover bowl loosely with plastic wrap. Let stand at room temperature 2 hours. If desired, refrigerate up to 7 days.

2. For each loaf, grease a 10- to 12-inch cast-iron skillet or a baking sheet; sprinkle generously with cornmeal. Using a sharp knife, cut off a third of the dough. (Place remaining dough in refrigerator.) Do not punch dough down. Place dough portion on a well-floured surface; sprinkle lightly with flour. Shape dough by gently pulling it into a ball, tucking edges underneath and adding additional flour as needed to keep dough from sticking to hands. Place in prepared skillet; sprinkle lightly with flour. Cover loosely with plastic wrap. Let rise in a warm place 20 minutes.

3. Preheat oven to 450°F. Score top of loaf with sharp knife. Place on middle oven rack; place a shallow roasting pan with 2 cups hot water on the rack below. Bake 25 to 30 minutes or until bread is deep golden brown. Remove from skillet; cool on a wire rack.

### Add-In (pick one)
Crumbled cooked bacon*
Shredded cheese
Snipped dried fruit
Sliced green onions
Chopped toasted nuts
Chopped pitted Kalamata olives
Chopped pepperoni*
Snipped dried tomatoes

*Note: If using bacon or pepperoni, serve baked bread within 2 hours or freeze for longer storage.

**PER SERVING** (1 slice each) **CAL** 93, **FAT** 0 g, **CHOL** 0 mg, **SODIUM** 151 mg, **CARB** 19 g (1 g fiber, 0 g sugars), **PRO** 3 g

**Wheat and Seed Loaf** Prepare as directed, except substitute 3 cups whole wheat flour for 3 cups of the all-purpose flour. Stir ¾ cup dry-roasted sunflower kernels and 3 Tbsp. each flaxseeds, sesame seeds, and poppy seeds into flour mixture.
**PER SLICE** Same as above, except **CAL** 120, **FAT** 3 g, **CARB** 20 g (3 g fiber), **PRO** 4 g

**Tip** If using chilled dough, increase rising time to 45 minutes.

**Tip** If desired, place a baking stone on the middle oven rack before preheating. After dough has risen, carefully transfer to the hot baking stone. Bake as directed.

### ⟫ QUICK TIP
The dough becomes stickier the longer it stands in the refrigerator. Take care not to overwork the sticky dough; you don't want to destroy the air pockets that have formed in the dough.

## Mixed-Grain Bread

**27 g**
**CARB**

| | |
|---|---|
| **SERVES** | 24 |
| **HANDS ON** | 30 min. |
| **TOTAL** | 2 hr. 40 min. |

3½ to 4 cups all-purpose flour
2 pkg. active dry yeast
1½ cups milk
¾ cup water
½ cup bulgur or cracked wheat
¼ cup cornmeal
¼ cup packed brown sugar*
3 Tbsp. vegetable or canola oil
2 tsp. salt
1½ cups whole wheat flour
½ cup rolled oats
1 egg white
1 tsp. water
Rolled oats

**1.** In a large bowl combine 2 cups of the all-purpose flour and the yeast. In a medium saucepan combine the next seven ingredients (through salt). Heat and stir over medium-low just until warm (120°F to 130°F). Add milk mixture to flour mixture. Beat with a mixer on low to medium 30 seconds, scraping sides of bowl. Beat on high 3 minutes. Stir in whole wheat flour, the ½ cup rolled oats, and as much of the remaining all-purpose flour as you can.

**2.** Turn dough out onto a lightly floured surface. Knead in enough of the remaining all-purpose flour to make a moderately stiff dough that is almost smooth and elastic (6 to 8 minutes total). Shape dough into a ball. Place in a lightly greased bowl, turning to coat dough. Cover; let rise in a warm place until double in size (about 1 hour).

**3.** Punch dough down. Turn out onto a lightly floured surface. Divide in half. Cover; let rest 10 minutes. Meanwhile, lightly grease two 8×4-inch loaf pans.

**4.** Shape each dough half into a loaf (tip, *opposite*). Place shaped dough halves in prepared pans. Cover; let rise in warm place until nearly double in size (about 30 minutes).

**5.** Preheat oven to 375°F. In a small bowl whisk together egg white and 1 Tbsp. *water*. Brush loaf tops with egg white mixture; sprinkle with additional rolled oats. Bake 30 to 35 minutes or until bread sounds hollow when lightly tapped. If necessary to prevent overbrowning, cover loosely with foil the last 10 minutes of baking. Immediately remove bread from pans. Cool on wire racks. Serve within 2 days or freeze for longer storage.

**PER SERVING** (*1 slice each*) **CAL** 147, **FAT** 3 g (0 g sat. fat), **CHOL** 1 mg, **SODIUM** 204 mg, **CARB** 27 g (2 g fiber, 3 g sugars), **PRO** 4 g

**\*Sugar Sub** Choose Splenda Brown Sugar Blend. Follow package directions to use ¼ cup equivalent.

**PER SERVING WITH SUB** Same as above, except **CAL** 144, **CARB** 26 g (2 g sugars)

**Tip** To pat dough into a loaf shape, use your hands to gently pat and pinch, tucking edges underneath. Place the shaped dough, seam side down, in prepared loaf pan. To roll dough into a loaf shape, use a rolling pin to form a 12×8-inch rectangle. Tightly roll up the rectangle, starting from a short side.

Pinch seam to seal. Place shaped dough, seam side down, in prepared loaf pan.

## Mock Sourdough Bread

**29 g**
**CARB**

**SERVES** 24
**HANDS ON** 45 min.
**TOTAL** 2 hr. 30 min.

6¾ to 7¼ cups all-purpose flour
1 pkg. active dry yeast
1½ cups water

3 Tbsp. sugar*
3 Tbsp. vegetable oil
2 tsp. salt
⅔ cup plain yogurt
2 Tbsp. lemon juice

**1.** In the bowl of an electric stand mixer combine 2½ cups of the flour and the yeast. In a 2-qt. saucepan heat and stir the water, sugar, oil, and salt just until warm (120°F to 130°F). Add water mixture, yogurt, and lemon juice to the flour mixture. Using a paddle attachment, beat on low to medium 30 seconds, scraping sides of bowl as needed. Beat on high

Mock Sourdough Bread

3 minutes, scraping sides of bowl occasionally. Stir in as much of the remaining flour as you can.

2. Turn dough out onto a lightly floured surface. Knead in enough remaining flour to make a moderately stiff dough that is smooth and elastic (6 to 8 minutes total). Shape dough into a ball. Place in a lightly greased bowl, turning to coat. Cover and let rise in a warm place until double in size (45 to 60 minutes).

3. Punch dough down. Turn out onto a lightly floured surface. Divide in half. Cover; let rest 10 minutes. Meanwhile, lightly grease two baking sheets.

4. Shape each dough half by gently pulling it into a ball, tucking edges under. Place dough rounds on prepared baking sheets. Flatten each round slightly to about 6 inches in diameter. Using a sharp knife, make an X in the top of each loaf. Cover and let rise in a warm place until nearly double in size (about 30 minutes).

5. Preheat oven to 375°F. Bake 30 to 35 minutes or until bread sounds hollow when lightly tapped. (A thermometer should register at least 200°F when inserted into centers of loaves.) If necessary, loosely cover with foil the last 10 minutes of baking to prevent overbrowning. Immediately remove bread from baking sheets. Cool on wire racks.

**PER SERVING** (1 slice each) **CAL** 155, **FAT** 2 g (0 g sat. fat), **CHOL** 0 mg, **SODIUM** 200 mg, **CARB** 29 g (1 g fiber, 2 g sugars), **PRO** 4 g

**\*Sugar Sub** We do not recommend a sugar sub for this recipe.

**To Store** Wrap cooled loaves tightly in plastic wrap. Store at room temperature up to 3 days. To freeze, place cooled loaves in resealable plastic freezer bags; seal. Freeze up to 2 months. Thaw wrapped bread at room temperature about 2 hours.

**Toasted Caraway and Rye Skillet Bread**

## Toasted Caraway and Rye Skillet Bread

**23 g CARB**

**SERVES** 8
**HANDS ON** 20 min.
**TOTAL** 40 min.

- 1 tsp. caraway seeds
- 1⅓ cups all-purpose flour
- ⅔ cup rye flour
- 1½ tsp. baking powder
- ¼ tsp. baking soda
- ¼ tsp. salt
- 2 Tbsp. cold butter
- 1 cup buttermilk
  Nonstick cooking spray

1. In a heavy 10-inch skillet cook caraway seeds over medium-low 3 to 5 minutes or until toasted, shaking skillet occasionally. Remove seeds from skillet. Set skillet aside to cool.
2. In a large bowl stir together toasted seeds and the next five ingredients (through salt). Using a pastry blender, cut in butter until mixture resembles coarse crumbs. Make a well in center of flour mixture. Add buttermilk all at once. Using a fork, stir just until moistened.

3. Turn dough out onto a well-floured surface. Knead 10 to 12 strokes until nearly smooth. Roll or pat dough into a 7-inch circle. Cut into eight wedges.

4. Coat skillet with cooking spray. Heat skillet over medium-low until a drop of water sizzles. Place dough wedges in hot pan.

5. Cook, covered, about 20 minutes or until golden and a toothpick comes out clean, turning wedges several times to brown both sides. Sides may still look moist. Check bottoms occasionally; if necessary to prevent overbrowning, reduce heat. Serve bread warm or at room temperature.

**PER SERVING** (1 wedge each) **CAL** 138, **FAT** 4 g (2 g sat. fat), **CHOL** 9 mg, **SODIUM** 210 mg, **CARB** 23 g (2 g fiber, 2 g sugars), **PRO** 4 g

Calico Blue
Corn Bread

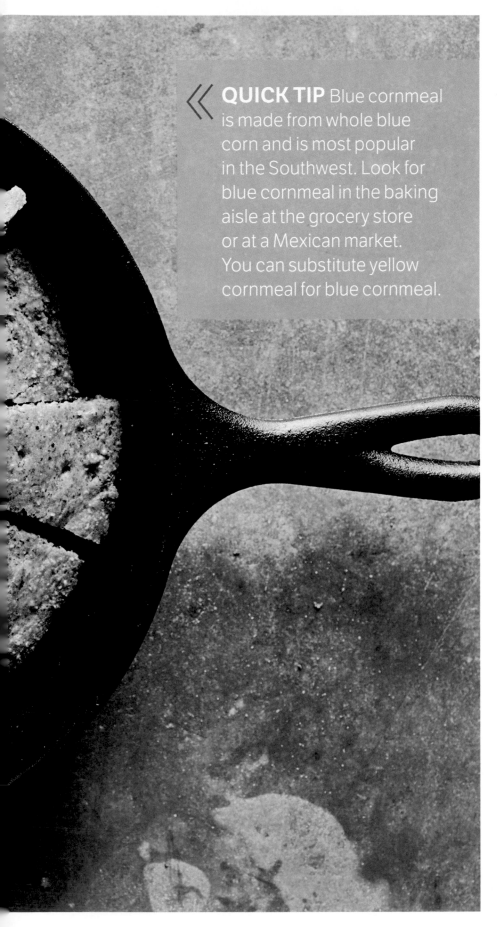

**QUICK TIP** Blue cornmeal is made from whole blue corn and is most popular in the Southwest. Look for blue cornmeal in the baking aisle at the grocery store or at a Mexican market. You can substitute yellow cornmeal for blue cornmeal.

## Calico Blue Corn Bread

**15 g**
CARB

**SERVES** 16
**HANDS ON** 15 min.
**TOTAL** 50 min.

- 2 eggs, lightly beaten
- ½ cup buttermilk
- 5 Tbsp. canola oil
- 2 Tbsp. honey
- 1 cup frozen fire-roasted corn
- 1 tsp. seeded and finely chopped fresh jalapeño chile pepper (tip, *p. 156*)
- 1 cup all-purpose flour
- ¾ cup blue cornmeal
- 1 tsp. salt
- 1 tsp. baking powder
- ¼ tsp. baking soda

**1.** Place a 10-inch cast-iron skillet in oven and preheat oven to 400°F.
**2.** In a small bowl combine eggs, buttermilk, 4 Tbsp. of the oil, and the honey. Stir in corn and jalapeño pepper. In a medium bowl stir together next five ingredients (through baking soda). Add egg mixture all at once to flour mixture; stir just until moistened.
**3.** Remove hot skillet from oven. Add remaining 1 Tbsp. oil to skillet, swirling to coat. Spread batter into prepared skillet. Bake 15 to 18 minutes or until top is golden and a toothpick comes out clean. Cool in skillet on a wire rack 20 to 30 minutes before serving.

**PER SERVING** *(1 wedge each)* **CAL** 120, **FAT** 5 g (1 g sat. fat), **CHOL** 24 mg, **SODIUM** 212 mg, **CARB** 15 g (1 g fiber, 3 g sugars), **PRO** 3 g

# 7

# FESTIVE
# ENDINGS

The holidays are a good time for showstopper desserts like Triple

Layer Pavlova. But you will also need cozy desserts perfect for

weeknight dinners and colorful fruit-based desserts that can star

on a brunch buffet. If you are looking for cookies to set out for drop-

in guests or to fill boxes for gift giving, we have those, too.

Mini Dark Chocolate-Mocha Mousses

**QUICK TIP** If you don't have a food processor, place the ingredients for the cream cheese mixture in a medium bowl and beat with a mixer on medium.

## Mini Dark Chocolate-Mocha Mousses

**24 g** CARB

**SERVES** 6
**HANDS ON** 25 min.
**TOTAL** 2 hr. 25 min.

- 7 chocolate wafer cookies, finely crushed
- 1½ tsp. butter, melted
- 1 tsp. honey
- 5 Tbsp. fat-free milk
- 1 Tbsp. instant espresso coffee powder
- 3 oz. reduced-fat cream cheese (neufchâtel)
- ⅓ cup unsweetened cocoa powder
- ¼ cup powdered sugar
- 3 Tbsp. dark chocolate pieces, melted
- 1½ Tbsp. plain fat-free Greek yogurt
- 2 tsp. vanilla
- ¾ cup frozen light whipped topping, thawed
- 12 fresh raspberries, halved
  Fresh mint leaves

**1.** In a bowl combine crushed cookies, melted butter, and honey (mixture will be crumbly). Using the handle of a wooden spoon, press half of the mixture onto bottoms of six 2-oz. shot glasses.
**2.** In another bowl stir together milk and espresso powder until dissolved. In a food processor combine milk mixture and the next six ingredients (through vanilla). Cover and process until smooth.
**3.** Fill a heavy resealable plastic bag with cream cheese mixture; snip off one corner of the bag. Pipe half of the mixture into shot glasses. Gently shake glasses side to side to spread mixture. Top with remaining crumb mixture and cream cheese mixture.
**4.** Cover and chill 2 to 24 hours. Before serving, top with whipped topping, raspberries, and mint.

**PER SERVING** (⅓ cup each) **CAL** 180, **FAT** 9 g (6 g sat. fat), **CHOL** 14 mg, **SODIUM** 107 mg, **CARB** 24 g (3 g fiber, 15 g sugars), **PRO** 4 g

## Peanut S'mores Cereal Bars

**20 g** CARB

**SERVES** 16
**HANDS ON** 15 min.
**TOTAL** 55 min.

  Nonstick cooking spray
- 3½ cups high-fiber cluster-style cereal, such as Fiber One Honey Clusters
- 1 egg white, lightly beaten
- 2 Tbsp. butter, melted
- ¾ cup miniature semisweet chocolate pieces, melted
- 1 cup tiny marshmallows
- ½ cup unsalted peanuts, toasted and coarsely chopped

**1.** Preheat oven to 350°F. Coat a 9-inch square baking pan with cooking spray.
**2.** Place cereal in a resealable plastic bag; seal bag. Using a rolling pin, very finely crush cereal. In a bowl combine cereal, egg white, and melted butter. Lightly press cereal mixture in the bottom of the prepared pan. Bake 10 to 12 minutes or until lightly browned.
**3.** Preheat broiler. Spread melted chocolate over crust. Top with marshmallows and peanuts. Broil 4 to 5 inches from heat 30 to 60 seconds or until lightly browned.
**4.** Place on wire rack and cool completely. Chill about 30 minutes or until firm. Cut into bars.

**PER SERVING** (1 bar each) **CAL** 140, **FAT** 7 g (3 g sal. fat), **CHOL** 4 mg, **SODIUM** 79 mg, **CARB** 20 g (3 g fiber, 9 g sugars), **PRO** 3 g

**To Store** Place bars in a single layer in an airtight container. Store in the refrigerator up to 3 days.

Peanut S'mores Cereal Bars

Pear-Pecan Crisp

## Pear-Pecan Crisp

**34 g**
**CARB**

**SERVES** 8
**HANDS ON** 20 min.
**TOTAL** 1 hr. 15 min.

6   medium pears
¼   cup pure maple syrup
2   Tbsp. white whole wheat flour
¼   tsp. ground nutmeg
¼   tsp. ground cardamom
⅛   tsp. salt
½   cup chopped pecans
⅓   cup rolled oats
2   Tbsp. butter, melted
2   Tbsp. pure maple syrup
¼   tsp. ground cinnamon
2   cups low-fat vanilla ice cream
    or frozen yogurt (optional)

**1.** Preheat oven to 375°F. Quarter, core, and thinly slice the pears. In a large bowl toss together pear slices and the ¼ cup maple syrup. Sprinkle with flour, nutmeg, cardamom, and salt. Toss to combine. Transfer mixture to a 2-qt. rectangular baking dish. Cover with foil; bake 10 minutes.
**2.** Meanwhile, in a medium bowl stir together pecans, oats, butter, the 2 Tbsp. syrup, and the cinnamon. Uncover pear mixture; spoon pecan mixture over partially cooked pears.
**3.** Bake, uncovered, 25 to 30 minutes or until filling is bubbly and topping is lightly browned. Cool in dish on a wire rack about 20 minutes. Serve warm. If desired, serve with ice cream.

**PER SERVING** (¾ cup each) **CAL** 201, **FAT** 8 g (2 g sat. fat), **CHOL** 8 mg, **SODIUM** 65 mg, **CARB** 34 g (5 g fiber, 23 g sugars), **PRO** 2 g

**Tip** The pears should be just ripe for best results. If desired, substitute 6 large cooking apples for the pears. In Step 1, increase the initial bake time for the apples to 20 minutes.

## Peanut Butter Blossom Mini Cakes

**9g** CARB

**SERVES** 20
**HANDS ON** 30 min.
**TOTAL** 45 min.

- ½ cup flour
- 3 Tbsp. ground lightly salted peanuts
- 1 tsp. baking powder
- ¼ cup creamy peanut butter
- ¼ cup sugar*
- ¼ cup refrigerated or frozen egg product, thawed, or 1 egg
- ½ tsp. vanilla
- ¼ cup fat-free milk
- 1 recipe Chocolate Frosting

**1.** Preheat oven to 375°F. Line twenty 1¾-inch muffin cups with paper bake cups. In a bowl combine flour, ground peanuts, and baking powder.

**2.** In another bowl beat peanut butter with a mixer on medium 30 seconds. Add sugar; beat until well combined. Beat in egg and vanilla. Alternately add flour mixture and milk, beating on low after each addition just until combined. Spoon 1 Tbsp. batter into each prepared muffin cup.

**3.** Bake 8 to 10 minutes or until a toothpick comes out clean. While warm, press the back of a measuring teaspoon into tops of cakes to flatten them. Cool cakes in cups on a wire rack 5 minutes; remove cakes. Cool. Pipe Chocolate Frosting on cakes.

**Chocolate Frosting** In a saucepan melt **⅓ cup butter** over low, stirring constantly. Stir in **⅓ cup unsweetened cocoa powder.** Remove from heat. Slowly beat in **2 cups powdered sugar, 1½ tsp. vanilla,** and **1 to 2 Tbsp. milk** to make a frosting creamy consistency.

**PER SERVING** *(1 mini cake each)* **CAL** 81, **FAT** 4 g (1 g sat. fat), **CHOL** 0 mg, **SODIUM** 53 mg, **CARB** 9 g (1 g fiber, 6 g sugars), **PRO** 2 g

**\*Sugar Sub** Choose Splenda Granular. Follow package directions to use ¼ cup equivalent.

**PER SERVING WITH SUB** Same as above, except **CAL** 72, **CARB** 7 g

**Peanut Butter Blossom Mini Cakes**

**Roasted Apples,
Grapes, and Cherries**

## Roasted Apples,
## Grapes, and Cherries

**30 g**
CARB

| | |
|---|---|
| **SERVES** 6 | |
| **HANDS ON** 20 min. | |
| **TOTAL** 45 min. | |

- 3 medium red cooking apples, cored and cut into 1-inch wedges
- 2 cups frozen unsweetened pitted dark sweet cherries
- 1 cup seedless red grapes
- 2 Tbsp. light butter with canola oil, melted
- 2 tsp. lemon juice
- 2 tsp. honey
- ½ tsp. ground cinnamon
- ¾ cup no-sugar-added vanilla ice cream
  Chopped pecans (optional)
  Fresh mint (optional)

**1.** Preheat oven to 375°F. In a 3-qt. rectangular baking dish combine apples, cherries, and grapes. In a small bowl combine melted butter, lemon juice, honey, and cinnamon. Drizzle mixture over fruit; toss to coat. Roast about 25 minutes or until tender, gently stirring once.

**2.** Serve roasted fruit with ice cream. If desired, top with pecans and mint.

**PER SERVING** *(¾ cup each)* **CAL** 145, **FAT** 3 g (1 g sat. fat), **CHOL** 11 mg, **SODIUM** 46 mg, **CARB** 30 g (4 g fiber, 23 g sugars), **PRO** 2 g

## Blood Oranges
## with Almond Syrup

**22 g**
CARB

| | |
|---|---|
| **SERVES** 4 | |
| **HANDS ON** 20 min. | |
| **TOTAL** 30 min. | |

- 3 blood oranges
- 1 Cara Cara orange
- ¾ cup quartered fresh strawberries
- 1 Tbsp. honey
- 1 Tbsp. amaretto (optional)
- ¼ tsp. almond extract
- 2 Tbsp. sliced almonds, toasted

**1.** Trim oranges and cut away peel and white pith. Thinly slice oranges. In a bowl stir together strawberries, honey, amaretto (if desired), and almond extract. Let stand 10 minutes.

**2.** Arrange oranges on a platter. Top with strawberry mixture and almonds.

**PER SERVING** *(⅓ cup each)* **CAL** 104, **FAT** 2 g (0 g sat. fat), **CHOL** 0 mg, **SODIUM** 1 mg, **CARB** 22 g (4 g fiber, 18 g sugars), **PRO** 2 g

**Blood Oranges
with Almond Syrup**

**Spiced-Pomegranate Poached Pears**

## Spiced-Pomegranate Poached Pears

**27 g**
**CARB**

| | |
|---|---|
| **SERVES** 4 | |
| **HANDS ON** 15 min. | |
| **TOTAL** 40 min. | |

- 1 cup dry red wine
- ½ cup pomegranate juice
- 1 Tbsp. sugar*
- 2 inches stick cinnamon
- 2 whole allspice
  Dash salt
- 2 8-oz. firm, ripe pears, peeled, halved lengthwise, and cored
- ½ tsp. vanilla
- ¼ cup chopped walnuts, toasted
  Ground cinnamon (optional)

**1.** In a 3-qt. saucepan combine the first six ingredients (through salt). Bring to boiling over medium. Add pear halves; reduce heat. Simmer, covered, 12 to 17 minutes or just until tender, turning pears three or four times. Remove from heat. Stir in vanilla. Remove pears, reserving cooking liquid. Cover pears and keep warm.

**2.** For syrup, remove and discard stick cinnamon and allspice. Bring cooking liquid to boiling; reduce heat. Boil gently, uncovered, about 5 minutes or until liquid is reduced to about 2 Tbsp.

**3.** To serve, drizzle pears with syrup and sprinkle with walnuts and, if desired, ground cinnamon.

**PER SERVING** (1 pear half each) **CAL** 193, **FAT** 5 g (0 g sat. fat), **CHOL** 0 mg, **SODIUM** 55 mg, **CARB** 27 g (4 g fiber, 19 g sugars), **PRO** 2 g

**\*Sugar Sub** We do not recommend a sugar sub for this recipe.

**Tip** To serve 8, double the ingredients and use a 5- to 6-qt. Dutch oven instead of a 3-qt. saucepan.

**Tip** To test the pears for doneness, insert a toothpick into the thickest part of a pear half. The pear should still be slightly firm, but the toothpick should penetrate easily.

## Cranberry Panna Cotta

**29 g** CARB

**SERVES** 4
**HANDS ON** 30 min.
**TOTAL** 4 hr. 30 min.

Nonstick cooking spray
1 vanilla bean, split lengthwise
½ cup fat-free half-and-half
1½ tsp. unflavored gelatin
1 cup plain fat-free Greek yogurt
½ cup fat-free milk
3 Tbsp. sugar*
2 Tbsp. water
⅛ tsp. salt
¾ cup fresh or frozen cranberries, coarsely chopped
⅓ cup 100% apple juice
2 to 3 Tbsp. sugar*
2 Tbsp. roasted and salted pistachio nuts, chopped

**1.** Coat four 8-oz. ramekins with cooking spray and place in a shallow baking pan or on a tray. Scrape seeds from vanilla bean. In a medium saucepan combine vanilla bean seeds and pod and half-and-half. Sprinkle with gelatin (do not stir); let stand 5 minutes. Cook and stir over medium-low until gelatin is dissolved. Whisk in the next five ingredients (through salt). Remove from heat. Remove and discard vanilla bean pod.
**2.** Pour mixture into the prepared ramekins. Cover and chill 4 hours or until firm.
**3.** Meanwhile, for cranberry sauce, in a 1- or 1½-qt. saucepan combine cranberries, apple juice, and 2 to 3 Tbsp. sugar. Bring to boiling; reduce heat to medium. Cook, uncovered, 5 to 8 minutes or until slightly thick, stirring occasionally. Cool.
**4.** Unmold panna cotta onto a platter or dessert plates. Top with cranberry sauce and pistachios.

**PER SERVING** (1 panna cotta each)
**CAL** 175, **FAT** 3 g (1 g sat. fat), **CHOL** 5 mg, **SODIUM** 156 mg, **CARB** 29 g (2 g fiber, 24 g sugars), **PRO** 10 g

**\*Sugar Sub** We do not recommend a sugar sub for this recipe.

Cranberry
Panna Cotta

**Tip** To unmold the panna cotta, loosen the edges from the sides of each ramekin with a sharp knife. Dip bottom of the ramekin into warm water 5 to 10 seconds, then invert onto a platter or dessert plate and remove the ramekin.

## Pumpkin Crème Brûlée

**23g**
**CARB**

**SERVES** 8
**HANDS ON** 20 min.
**TOTAL** 9 hr. 10 min.

 1  12-oz. can evaporated
    fat-free milk
 ¾  cup half-and-half
 1  Tbsp. butter
 ¾  tsp. pumpkin pie spice
 ¼  tsp. salt
 4  egg yolks
 1  egg
 ¾  cup canned pumpkin
 ⅓  cup sugar*
 1½  tsp. vanilla
 8  tsp. sugar*
 ½  cup frozen light whipped
    topping, thawed

**1.** Preheat oven to 325°F. Place eight 6-oz. ramekins or custard cups in a large roasting pan. In a 1- to 1½- heavy saucepan heat the first five ingredients (through salt) over medium-low just until edges are bubbly and butter is nearly melted.

**2.** Meanwhile, in a medium bowl beat egg yolks, egg, pumpkin, ⅓ cup sugar, and vanilla with a whisk just until combined. Slowly whisk in the hot milk mixture.

**3.** Divide pumpkin mixture among ramekins. Place roasting pan on oven rack. Pour enough boiling water into roasting pan to reach halfway up sides of ramekins.

**4.** Bake 30 to 40 minutes or until centers barely move when pan is touched. Remove ramekins from water; cool on a wire rack. Cover and chill at least 8 hours or overnight.

**5.** Before serving, let custards stand at room temperature 20 minutes. Meanwhile, in an 8-inch heavy skillet heat 8 tsp. sugar over medium-high until sugar begins to melt, shaking skillet occasionally (do not stir). Once the sugar starts to melt, reduce heat to low and cook 5 minutes or until all of the sugar is melted and golden, stirring as needed with a wooden spoon.

**6.** Quickly pour melted sugar over custards. (If sugar hardens in the skillet, return to heat; stir until melted.) Serve immediately with whipped topping.

**PER SERVING** *(1 custard each)* **CAL** 182, **FAT** 7 g (4 g sat. fat), **CHOL** 127 mg, **SODIUM** 169 mg, **CARB** 23 g (1 g fiber, 21 g sugars), **PRO** 6 g

**\*Sugar Sub** Use Splenda Blend for Baking for the custards. Follow package directions to use ⅓ cup equivalent. Use regular sugar for the topping.

**PER SERVING WITH SUB** Same as original, except **CAL** 169, **CARB** 19 g (16 g sugars)

**Tip** To use a kitchen torch, prepare as directed through Step 4. Let custards stand at room temperature 20 minutes. Sprinkle 1 tsp. of the sugar over each custard. Melt the sugar by evenly moving the tip of the flame across the tops of the custards to form a crispy layer.

Pumpkin
Crème Brûlée

## Marshmallow
## Sweet Potato Bars

**20 g**
**CARB**

| **SERVES** 16 |
| **HANDS ON** 15 min. |
| **TOTAL** 35 min. |

**Nonstick cooking spray**

2  **6.4-oz. pkg. banana nut muffin mix**

½  **cup refrigerated or frozen egg product, thawed, or 2 eggs, lightly beaten**

⅓  **cup water**

⅓  **cup mashed sweet potatoes**

¼  **cup canola oil**

1  **tsp. vanilla**

1  **cup tiny marshmallows**

16  **pecan halves, toasted**

**1.** Preheat oven to 400°F. Coat a 9-inch square baking pan with cooking spray.

**2.** In a bowl stir together the next six ingredients (through vanilla) until smooth. Spread batter in the prepared pan.

**3.** Bake about 18 minutes or until a toothpick inserted near the center comes out clean. Sprinkle marshmallows over the top. Bake 2 to 3 minutes more or until marshmallows are puffed and golden brown. Top with pecan halves. Cool in pan on a wire rack. Cut into bars.

**PER SERVING** (1 bar each) **CAL** 145, **FAT** 6 g (1 g sat. fat), **CHOL** 0 mg, **SODIUM** 170 mg, **CARB** 20 g (1 g fiber, 10 g sugars), **PRO** 2 g

**QUICK TIP** Any extra filling can be placed in custard cups and chilled for individual desserts.

**Butternut-Mascarpone Chiffon Pie**

## Butternut-Mascarpone Chiffon Pie

**27 g**
**CARB**

| | |
|---|---|
| **SERVES** | 10 |
| **HANDS ON** | 30 min. |
| **TOTAL** | 4 hr. 45 min. |

- 1 recipe Baked Graham Cracker Piecrust *(opposite)*
- 1 envelope unflavored gelatin
- ½ cup cold water
- ¼ cup packed brown sugar*

- 1 12-oz. pkg. frozen cooked winter squash, thawed
- 1 tsp. vanilla
- ½ tsp. pumpkin pie spice
- ⅓ cup mascarpone cheese or reduced-fat cream cheese, softened
- ½ cup refrigerated pasteurized egg whites
- ¼ tsp. cream of tartar
- ¼ cup granulated sugar*

Frozen light whipped dessert topping, thawed (optional)

**1.** Prepare Baked Graham Cracker Piecrust.

**2.** In a 1- to 1½-qt. saucepan sprinkle gelatin over the water. Let stand 5 minutes. Add brown sugar. Cook and stir over medium until gelatin and sugar are dissolved. Remove from heat; let cool 10 minutes.

**3.** Meanwhile, in a bowl combine squash, vanilla, and pumpkin pie spice. Using a rubber spatula, gently stir in mascarpone until combined. Stir in gelatin mixture.

**4.** In another bowl combine egg whites and cream of tartar. Beat with a mixer on high until soft peaks form (tips curl). Gradually beat in granulated sugar, 1 tsp. at a time, until stiff peaks form (tips stand straight). Fold about 1 cup of the egg whites into squash mixture to lighten. Very gently fold in remaining egg whites.

**5.** Pour about 4 cups of the squash mixture into cooled crust, spreading evenly. Cover loosely with plastic wrap. Chill at least 4 hours or up to 8 hours before serving. If desired, top each serving with a small spoonful of whipped topping and sprinkle with additional pumpkin pie spice.

**Baked Graham Cracker Piecrust**
Preheat oven to 375°F. In a bowl stir together **1 cup crushed graham crackers (16 squares)** and **2 Tbsp. packed brown sugar.*** Stir in **3 Tbsp. melted butter** until crumbs are evenly coated. Press crumbs onto bottom and up sides of a 9-inch pie plate. Bake 5 to 8 minutes or until edges are light brown. Cool on a wire rack.

**PER SERVING** (1 wedge each) **CAL** 190, **FAT** 8 g (4 g sat. fat), **CHOL** 20 mg, **SODIUM** 100 mg, **CARB** 27 g (1 g fiber, 17 g sugars), **PRO** 3 g

***Sugar Sub** We do not recommend sugar subs for this recipe.

### Hazelnut Cream Puffs with Chocolate-Banana Filling

**16 g**
**CARB**

**SERVES** 12
**HANDS ON** 20 min.
**TOTAL** 3 hr. 25 min.

- 1 recipe Chocolate-Banana Filling
  Nonstick cooking spray
- 1 cup water
- ¼ cup butter
- ⅛ tsp. salt

- ¾ cup all-purpose flour
- ¼ cup toasted, coarsely ground hazelnuts
- 4 eggs
- 2 large bananas (optional)

**1.** Prepare Chocolate-Banana Filling. Preheat oven to 400°F. Lightly coat a large baking sheet with cooking spray. In a 2-qt. saucepan combine water, butter, and salt. Bring to boiling. Add flour and hazelnuts all at once, stirring vigorously. Cook and stir until mixture forms a ball. Remove from heat. Cool 10 minutes. Add eggs, one at a time, beating well with a wooden spoon after each addition.

**2.** Drop 12 mounds of dough (about 3 Tbsp. each) onto the prepared baking sheet. Bake 25 to 30 minutes or until golden brown and firm. Remove; cool on a wire rack.

**3.** Cut tops from puffs; remove soft dough from inside. Spoon Chocolate-Banana Filling evenly into puff bottoms. Replace tops. If using bananas, split bananas in half lengthwise. Lay banana halves, cut sides down, on a cutting board. Using a 1-inch star cookie cutter, cut as many stars from the bananas as you can. Add the stars to the filled cream puffs.

**Chocolate-Banana Filling** In a bowl combine 7 **unsweetened pitted whole dates** and ½ cup boiling water. Cover; let stand 15 minutes. Meanwhile, in a 1- to 1½-qt. saucepan sprinkle **2 tsp. gelatin** over ½ cup fat-free milk. Let stand 5 minutes. Add **2 Tbsp. sugar;*** cook and stir over medium until sugar and gelatin are dissolved. Remove from heat; cool 10 minutes. In a blender or food processor, combine undrained dates; milk mixture; **1 medium banana, peeled and halved; 1 small avocado, halved, seeded, and peeled;** and **3 Tbsp. unsweetened cocoa powder.** Cover and blend until smooth, scraping blender as needed. Transfer mixture to a bowl. Cover the surface with plastic wrap. Chill at least 2 hours or up to 24 hours.

**PER SERVING** (1 cream puff each) **CAL** 152, **FAT** 8 g (3 g sat. fat), **CHOL** 72 mg, **SODIUM** 85 mg, **CARB** 16 g (2 g fiber, 7 g sugars), **PRO** 5 g

***Sugar Sub** We do not recommend a sugar sub for this recipe.

Hazelnut Cream Puffs with Chocolate-Banana Filling

## Triple-Layer Pavlova with Cherry-Berry Sauce

**30 g CARB**

| | |
|---|---|
| **SERVES** | 14 |
| **HANDS ON** | 45 min. |
| **TOTAL** | 3 hr. 20 min. |

- 4 egg whites, room temperature
- 1 tsp. vanilla
- ¼ tsp. cream of tartar
- 1¼ cups sugar*
- ¼ cup finely chopped toasted slivered almonds
- 2 Tbsp. unsweetened cocoa powder
- 1 recipe Orange-Mascarpone Cream
- 1 recipe Cherry-Berry Sauce
- 2 oz. semisweet chocolate, chopped
- 2 Tbsp. fat-free half-and-half

**1.** Preheat oven to 300°F. Line two extra-large baking sheets with parchment paper or foil. Draw an 8-inch circle on one sheet of paper. Draw two 8-inch circles on the other sheet of paper, leaving about 1 inch between circles.

**2.** In a large bowl combine egg whites, vanilla, and cream of tartar. Beat with a mixer on medium until soft peaks form (tips curl). Gradually add the 1¼ cups sugar, 1 Tbsp. at a time, beating on high about 5 minutes or until stiff peaks form (tips stand straight) and sugar is nearly dissolved.

**3.** Spoon about one-third of the meringue onto one of the circles on the baking sheets, spreading evenly to edge of circle. Spoon about half of the remaining meringue into a bowl. Fold in almonds. Spoon almond meringue onto another circle on baking sheet, spreading evenly to edge of circle. Sift the cocoa powder over the remaining meringue; fold in thoroughly. (Cocoa meringue will deflate a little.) Spoon onto remaining circle, spreading evenly to edge of circle.

**4.** Bake all of the meringues at the same time with sheets on separate oven racks 35 minutes. Turn off oven; let meringues dry in oven with door closed 1 hour.

**5.** To assemble, carefully lift meringues off paper. Place one meringue on a round platter. Spread with one-third of the Orange-Mascarpone Cream. Top with one-third of the Cherry-Berry Sauce. Repeat layers twice. Cover loosely and chill 1 to 2 hours.

**6.** In a bowl combine chocolate and half-and-half. Microwave on 50% power (medium) 1 to 2 minutes or until chocolate is melted and smooth, stirring once or twice. Drizzle over pavlova. Cut pavlova into wedges. Serve immediately.

**Orange-Mascarpone Cream**
Remove ½ **tsp. zest** and squeeze ¼ **cup juice from orange.** In a bowl beat **half of an 8-oz. carton mascarpone cheese** with a mixer on medium until smooth. Beat in orange zest; gradually beat in orange juice until well combined. Fold in **1½ cups frozen light whipped dessert topping, thawed.**

**Cherry-Berry Sauce** Place ⅓ **cup frozen unsweetened pitted tart red cherries** in a bowl to thaw. Do not drain. Use kitchen scissors to coarsely snip cherries. In a medium saucepan combine **3 Tbsp. sugar*** and **1 Tbsp. cornstarch.** Stir in ¾ **cup water** until well combined. Add ⅓ **cup cranberries, coarsely chopped,** and the undrained cherries. Cook and stir over medium until thickened and bubbly. Cook and stir 2 minutes more. Remove from heat. Let cool 10 minutes. Stir in **1 cup coarsely chopped fresh strawberries.**

**PER SERVING** *(1 wedge each)* **CAL** 182, **FAT** 7 g (4 g sat. fat), **CHOL** 12 mg, **SODIUM** 22 mg, **CARB** 30 g (1 g fiber, 25 g sugars), **PRO** 2 g

*****Sugar Sub** We do not recommend a sugar sub for this recipe.

## Sugar Cookie Cutouts

**16 g CARB**

**SERVES** 45
**HANDS ON** 1 hr.
**TOTAL** 2 hr. 30 min.

- ⅔ cup butter, softened
- ¾ cup granulated sugar*
- 1 tsp. baking powder
- ¼ tsp. salt
- 1 egg
- 1 Tbsp. fat-free milk
- 1 tsp. vanilla
- 2 cups all-purpose flour
- 1 recipe Royal Icing

**1.** In a large bowl beat butter with a mixer on medium 30 seconds. Add granulated sugar, baking powder, and salt. Beat until combined, scraping bowl as needed. Beat in egg, milk, and vanilla. Beat in flour. Divide dough in half. Shape halves into disks. Wrap in plastic wrap and chill 1 hour or until easy to handle.

**2.** Preheat oven to 375°F. On a lightly floured surface, roll one portion of dough at a time until ⅛ inch thick. Using a 2¾- to 3-inch cookie cutter, cut out desired shapes. Place cutouts 1 inch apart on an ungreased cookie sheet.

**3.** Bake 7 to 10 minutes or until edges are firm and bottoms are very light brown. Remove; cool cookies on a wire rack. Decorated as desired with Royal Icing.

**Royal Icing** In a large bowl stir together **3 cups powdered sugar,* 2 Tbsp. plus ¾ tsp. meringue powder,** and **½ tsp. cream of tartar.** Add **6 Tbsp. warm water** and **¾ tsp. vanilla.** Beat with a mixer on low until combined. Beat on high 7 to 10 minutes or until icing is very stiff. If not using immediately, cover bowl with a damp paper towel; cover tightly with plastic wrap (icing will dry out quickly when exposed to air). Chill up to 48 hours. Stir before using. Makes about 3 cups.

**PER SERVING** (1 cookie each) **CAL** 91, **FAT** 3 g (2 g sat. fat), **CHOL** 11 mg, **SODIUM** 48 mg, **CARB** 16 g (0 g fiber, 11 g sugars), **PRO** 1 g

**\*Sugar Sub** We do not recommend sugar subs for this recipe.

**To Store** Layer unfrosted cookies between waxed paper in an airtight container; cover. Store at room temperature up to 3 days or freeze up to 3 months.

### OMBRÉ EFFECT
Frost cookies with Royal Icing; let set. In small bowls mix food coloring with enough water to achieve desired shades. Use a clean ¾-inch brush to paint frosting with food coloring mixture. Let dry. If desired, use a smaller brush to paint on gold or silver luster dust for sparkle.

### SHIMMERING TREES
Brush cookies with luster dust. Fill a pastry bag (or resealable plastic bag) with Royal Icing and pipe trees onto cookies. Top each tree with a decorative candy ball. Let dry. Brush on more luster dust.

### COCOA SNOWFLAKES
Create a stencil with desired design (we chose snowflakes!). Reserve the inside and outside portions to create two designs. Place stencil on top of cookie. Fill a fine-mesh sieve with cocoa powder. Lightly shake sieve over cookie. Gently lift stencil to reveal design.

**Sugar Cookie Cutouts**

**Almond Spirals**

## Almond Spirals

**6g**
**CARB**

**SERVES** 70
**HANDS ON** 30 min.
**TOTAL** 4 hr. 40 min.

¾  cup butter, softened
1  cup sugar*
½  tsp. baking powder
¼  tsp. salt
1  egg
1  tsp. vanilla
½  tsp. almond extract
2  cups all-purpose flour
    Red paste food coloring
¼  cup ground almonds

**1.** In a large bowl beat butter with a mixer on medium to high 30 seconds. Add sugar, baking powder, and salt. Beat until combined, scraping sides of bowl occasionally. Beat in egg, vanilla, and almond extract until combined. Beat in as much of the flour as you can with the mixer. Stir in any remaining flour.

**2.** Divide dough in half. Tint one portion of dough using red food coloring. Stir or knead ground almonds into the remaining dough portion. Cover each portion and chill about 1 hour or until dough is easy to handle. Divide each portion in half.

**3.** Between two sheets of waxed paper, roll one portion of the red dough into 12×8-inch rectangle. Repeat, using one potion of almond dough. Remove the top sheets of waxed paper. Invert one rectangle on top of the other; press together gently to seal. Remove the remaining sheet of waxed paper. Tightly roll up rectangle, starting from a long side; pinch seam to seal. Repeat with the remaining dough portions. Wrap each roll in waxed paper or plastic wrap. Chill about 3 hours or until dough is firm enough to slice.

**4.** Preheat oven to 375°F. Lightly grease a cookie sheet. Using a sharp knife, cut rolls into ¼-inch slices. Place slices 2 inches apart on the prepared cookie sheet. Bake 8 minutes or until tops are set. Cool on cookie sheet 1 minute. Transfer to wire rack; cool.

**PER SERVING** *(1 cookie each)* **CAL** 45, **FAT** 2 g (1 g sat. fat), **CHOL** 8 mg, **SODIUM** 30 mg, **CARB** 6 g (0 g fiber, 3 g sugars), **PRO** 1 g

**\*Sugar Sub** We do not recommend a sugar sub for this recipe.

**To Store** Layer cookies between sheets of waxed paper in an airtight container; cover. Store at room temperature up to 3 days or freeze up to 3 months.

Chocolate Snowball Cookies

## Chocolate Snowball Cookies

**11 g**
**CARB**

**SERVES** 48
**HANDS ON** 25 min.
**TOTAL** 1 hr. 10 min.

- 1 **cup butter, softened**
- ½ **cup powdered sugar\***
- ¼ **cup unsweetened dark cocoa powder**
- 1 **tsp. vanilla**
- 1 **tsp. orange zest**
- ½ **tsp. salt**
- 2¼ **cups all-purpose flour**
- 1 **cup miniature semisweet chocolate pieces**
- 1 **cup powdered sugar\***

**1.** In a large bowl beat butter with a mixer on medium to high 30 seconds. Add the next five ingredients (through salt). Beat until combined, scraping bowl as needed. Beat in flour. Stir in chocolate pieces (dough will be crumbly). Use hands to knead dough and shape into a ball. Cover dough and chill 30 to 60 minutes or until easy to handle.
**2.** Preheat oven to 325°F. Shape dough into 1-inch balls. Place dough balls 1 inch apart on ungreased cookie sheets. Bake about 15 minutes or until cookies are just firm and tops are no longer glossy. Remove; cool on wire racks.
**3.** Place the 1 cup powdered sugar in a large plastic bag. Add cooled cookies in batches to bag. Gently shake to coat.

**PER SERVING** *(1 cookie each)* **CAL** 88, **FAT** 5 g (3 g sat. fat), **CHOL** 10 mg, **SODIUM** 61 mg, **CARB** 11 g (1 g fiber, 6 g sugars), **PRO** 1 g

**\*Sugar Sub** We do not recommend a sugar sub for this recipe.

**To Store** Arrange cookies in a single layer in an airtight container; cover. Store at room temperature up to 3 days or freeze up to 3 months.

## Vanilla Cookie Dough

**TOTAL** 15 min.

- 1 **cup butter, softened**
- ⅔ **cup sugar***
- ½ **tsp. salt**
- 1 **egg**
- 1 **Tbsp. vanilla**
- 2 **cups all-purpose flour**

**1.** In a large bowl beat butter with a mixer on medium to high 30 seconds. Add the sugar and salt. Beat on medium 2 minutes, scraping bowl as needed. Beat in egg and vanilla. Beat in flour until combined. Divide dough into three portions.

***Sugar Sub** We do not recommend a sugar sub for this recipe.

**Vanilla Cookie Dough**

Pistachio-Cranberry
Stick Dough

Chai-Spiced
Pine Cone
Dough

Mint-Ganache
Sandwich
Cookie Dough

《 **QUICK TIP** With one batch of Vanilla Cookie
Dough *(left)*, you can fill a cookie platter with a
variety of cookies. See recipes on *p. 155.*

**Mint-Ganache
Sandwich Cookies**

**Chai-Spiced
Pine Cones**

**Pistachio-Cranberry Sticks**

## Mint-Ganache Sandwich Cookies

**13 g**
CARB

| | |
|---|---|
| **SERVES** | 18 |
| **HANDS ON** | 25 min. |
| **TOTAL** | 1 hr. |

- 1 portion Vanilla Cookie Dough (p. 152)
- 2 Tbsp. heavy cream
- ¼ cup miniature semisweet chocolate pieces
- ⅔ cup powdered sugar*
- 1 Tbsp. butter, softened
- 2 tsp. milk
- ¼ tsp. mint extract
- 1 drop green food coloring

**1.** Wrap and chill dough 30 to 60 minutes or until easy to handle. Preheat oven to 375°F. On a lightly floured surface roll dough to a 9-inch square. Using a pastry wheel, cut dough into 1½-inch squares. Arrange dough squares 2 inches apart on an ungreased cookie sheet. Prick each several times with a fork. Bake 6 to 8 minutes or until edges are lightly browned. Cool on cookie sheet 1 minute. Remove; cool on wire racks.
**2.** For ganache, in a small bowl microwave cream 20 to 30 seconds or just until boiling. Add chocolate (do not stir). Let stand 5 minutes. Stir until smooth. Chill 10 minutes or until spreadable.
**3.** For mint frosting, in a small bowl stir together powdered sugar, butter, milk, and mint extract until spreading consistency. Add food coloring.
**4.** Spread frosting on the bottoms of half of the cookies. Spread ganache on bottoms of remaining cookies; chill 10 minutes to set. Top ganache-topped cookies with frosting-topped cookies. Lightly dust cookies with additional powdered sugar.

**PER SERVING** (1 sandwich cookie each) **CAL** 107, **FAT** 6 g (4 g sat. fat), **CHOL** 16 mg, **SODIUM** 56 mg, **CARB** 13 g (0 g fiber, 9 g sugars), **PRO** 1 g

**\*Sugar Sub** We do not recommend a sugar sub for this recipe.

**To Store** Layer filled cookies between sheets of waxed paper in an airtight container; cover. Store in refrigerator up to 3 days or freeze up to 3 months.

## Chai-Spiced Pine Cones

**8 g**
CARB

| | |
|---|---|
| **SERVES** | 18 |
| **HANDS ON** | 30 min. |
| **TOTAL** | 1 hr. 10 min. |

- 1½ tsp. Chai Spice
- 1 portion Vanilla Cookie Dough (p. 152)
- ¼ cup sliced almonds
- 2 oz. bittersweet or semisweet chocolate, chopped
- ½ tsp. shortening
  Powdered sugar* (optional)

**1.** Stir Chai Spice into dough portion. Wrap and chill dough 30 to 60 minutes or until easy to handle. Preheat oven to 375°F. On a lightly floured surface roll dough to ¼ inch thick. Using a 2-inch teardrop-shape or oval cookie cutter, cut out dough. Arrange cutouts 2 inches apart on an ungreased cookie sheet. Insert almonds on cutouts at an angle to resemble a pine cone, leaving about ½ inch at the bottoms.
**2.** Bake 8 to 10 minutes or until edges start to brown. Cool on cookie sheet 1 minute. Remove; cool on wire racks.
**3.** Place chocolate and shortening in a bowl. Microwave about 1 minute or until melted and smooth, stirring once. Dip the bottom of each pine cone into melted chocolate mixture. Let stand until set. If desired, lightly sprinkle with powdered sugar.

**Chai Spice** In a small bowl stir together **1 tsp. ground cardamom**, **¼ tsp. each ground ginger** and **ground cinnamon**, and **dash ground cloves**.

**PER SERVING** (1 cookie each) **CAL** 84, **FAT** 6 g (3 g sat. fat), **CHOL** 12 mg, **SODIUM** 50 mg, **CARB** 8 g (1 g fiber, 4 g sugars), **PRO** 1 g

**\*Sugar Sub** We do not recommend a sugar sub for this recipe.

**To Store** Layer cookies between sheets of waxed paper in an airtight container; cover. Store in the refrigerator up to 3 days or freeze up to 3 months.

## Pistachio-Cranberry Sticks

**9 g**
CARB

| | |
|---|---|
| **SERVES** | 24 |
| **HANDS ON** | 25 min. |
| **TOTAL** | 1 hr. 5 min. |

- ½ cup finely chopped pistachio nuts
- ¼ cup dried cranberries, finely chopped
- 1 portion Vanilla Cookie Dough (p. 152)
- ½ cup white baking pieces
- 1 tsp. shortening
- 1 tsp. tangerine or orange zest

**1.** Stir pistachios and cranberries into dough portion. Cover and chill dough 30 to 60 minutes or until easy to handle. Preheat oven to 375°F. On a lightly floured surface roll the dough to an 8×6-inch rectangle about ½ inch thick. Cut lengthwise into eight ¾-inch-wide strips. Cut each into thirds crosswise. Place pieces 1 inch apart on an ungreased cookie sheet.
**2.** Bake about 8 minutes or until edges start to brown. Cool on cookie sheet 1 minute. Remove; cool on wire racks.
**3.** Place baking pieces and shortening in a small bowl. Microwave about 1 minute or until melted and smooth, stirring once. Dip ends of cookie sticks into melted chocolate to coat. Place on waxed paper; sprinkle white chocolate with zest and, if desired, additional finely chopped pistachios and/or dried cranberries. Let stand or chill until set.

**PER SERVING** (1 cookie each) **CAL** 91, **FAT** 5 g (3 g sat. fat), **CHOL** 9 mg, **SODIUM** 56 mg, **CARB** 9 g (0 g fiber, 6 g sugars), **PRO** 1 g

**To Store** Layer cookies between sheets of waxed paper in an airtight container; cover. Store in the refrigerator up to 3 days or freeze up to 3 months.

# RECIPE GUIDE

## High-standards testing

This seal assures you that every recipe in *Diabetic Living® Holiday Cooking* has been tested by the Better Homes & Gardens® Diabetic Living® Test Kitchen. This means each recipe is practical, reliable, and meets our high standards of taste appeal.

## Inside Our Recipes

Precise serving sizes (listed below the recipe title) help you to manage portions.

Ingredients listed as optional are not included in the per-serving nutrition analysis.

When kitchen basics such as ice, salt, black pepper, and nonstick cooking spray are not listed in the ingredients list, they are italicized in the directions.

### Ingredients
- Tub-style vegetable oil spread refers to 60% to 70% vegetable oil product.
- Lean ground beef refers to 95% or leaner ground beef.

## Nutrition Information

Nutrition facts per serving are noted with each recipe.

Test Kitchen tips and sugar substitutes are listed after the recipe directions.

When ingredient choices appear, we use the first one to calculate the nutrition analysis.

## Key to Abbreviations
**CAL** = calories
**sat. fat** = saturated fat
**CHOL** = cholesterol
**CARB** = carbohydrate
**PRO** = protein

## Test Kitchen tip

### Handling hot chile peppers
Chile peppers can irritate skin and eyes. Wear gloves when working with them. If your bare hands do touch the peppers, wash your hands with soap and warm water.

# RECIPE INDEX

# METRIC INFORMATION

The charts on this page provide a guide for converting measurements from the U.S. customary system, which is used throughout this book, to the metric system.

## Product Differences

Most of the ingredients called for in the recipes in this book are available in most countries. However, some are known by different names. Here are some common American ingredients and their possible counterparts:

* All-purpose flour is enriched, bleached or unbleached white household flour. When self-rising flour is used in place of all-purpose flour in a recipe that calls for leavening, omit the leavening agent (baking soda or baking powder) and salt.
* Baking soda is bicarbonate of soda.
* Cornstarch is cornflour.
* Golden raisins are sultanas.
* Light-color corn syrup is golden syrup.
* Powdered sugar is icing sugar.
* Sugar (white) is granulated, fine granulated, or castor sugar.
* Vanilla or vanilla extract is vanilla essence.

## Volume and Weight

The United States traditionally uses cup measures for liquid and solid ingredients. The chart below shows the approximate imperial and metric equivalents. If you are accustomed to weighing solid ingredients, the following approximate equivalents will be helpful.

* 1 cup butter, castor sugar, or rice = 8 ounces = $\frac{1}{2}$ pound = 250 grams
* 1 cup flour = 4 ounces = $\frac{1}{4}$ pound = 125 grams
* 1 cup icing sugar = 5 ounces = 150 grams

Canadian and U.S. volume for a cup measure is 8 fluid ounces (237 ml), but the standard metric equivalent is 250 ml.

1 British imperial cup is 10 fluid ounces.

In Australia, 1 tablespoon equals 20 ml, and there are 4 teaspoons in the Australian tablespoon.

Spoon measures are used for smaller amounts of ingredients. Although the size of the tablespoon varies slightly in different countries, for practical purposes and for recipes in this book, a straight substitution is all that's necessary. Measurements made using cups or spoons always should be level unless stated otherwise.

## Common Weight Range Replacements

| Imperial / U.S. | Metric |
|---|---|
| $\frac{1}{2}$ ounce | 15 g |
| 1 ounce | 25 g or 30 g |
| 4 ounces ($\frac{1}{4}$ pound) | 115 g or 125 g |
| 8 ounces ($\frac{1}{2}$ pound) | 225 g or 250 g |
| 16 ounces (1 pound) | 450 g or 500 g |
| $1\frac{1}{4}$ pounds | 625 g |
| $1\frac{1}{2}$ pounds | 750 g |
| 2 pounds or $2\frac{1}{4}$ pounds | 1,000 g or 1 Kg |

## Oven Temperature Equivalents

| Fahrenheit Setting | Celsius Setting* | Gas Setting |
|---|---|---|
| 300°F | 150°C | Gas Mark 2 (very low) |
| 325°F | 160°C | Gas Mark 3 (low) |
| 350°F | 180°C | Gas Mark 4 (moderate) |
| 375°F | 190°C | Gas Mark 5 (moderate) |
| 400°F | 200°C | Gas Mark 6 (hot) |
| 425°F | 220°C | Gas Mark 7 (hot) |
| 450°F | 230°C | Gas Mark 8 (very hot) |
| 475°F | 240°C | Gas Mark 9 (very hot) |
| 500°F | 260°C | Gas Mark 10 (extremely hot) |
| Broil | Broil | Grill |

*Electric and gas ovens may be calibrated using celsius. However, for an electric oven, increase celsius setting 10 to 20 degrees when cooking above 160°C. For convection or forced air ovens (gas or electric), lower the temperature setting 25°F/10°C when cooking at all heat levels.*

## Baking Pan Sizes

| Imperial / U.S. | Metric |
|---|---|
| 9×1$\frac{1}{2}$-inch round cake pan | 22- or 23×4-cm (1.5 L) |
| 9×1$\frac{1}{2}$-inch pie plate | 22- or 23×4-cm (1 L) |
| 8×8×2-inch square cake pan | 20×5-cm (2 L) |
| 9×9×2-inch square cake pan | 22- or 23×4.5-cm (2.5 L) |
| 11×7×1$\frac{1}{2}$-inch baking pan | 28×17×4-cm (2 L) |
| 2-quart rectangular baking pan | 30×19×4.5-cm (3 L) |
| 13×9×2-inch baking pan | 34×22×4.5-cm (3.5 L) |
| 15×10×1-inch jelly roll pan | 40×25×2-cm |
| 9×5×3-inch loaf pan | 23×13×8-cm (2 L) |
| 2-quart casserole | 2 L |

## U.S. / Standard Metric Equivalents

| | |
|---|---|
| $\frac{1}{8}$ teaspoon = 0.5 ml | |
| $\frac{1}{4}$ teaspoon = 1 ml | |
| $\frac{1}{2}$ teaspoon = 2 ml | |
| 1 teaspoon = 5 ml | |
| 1 tablespoon = 15 ml | |
| 2 tablespoons = 25 ml | |
| $\frac{1}{4}$ cup = 2 fluid ounces = 50 ml | |
| $\frac{1}{3}$ cup = 3 fluid ounces = 75 ml | |
| $\frac{1}{2}$ cup = 4 fluid ounces = 125 ml | |
| $\frac{2}{3}$ cup = 5 fluid ounces = 150 ml | |
| $\frac{3}{4}$ cup = 6 fluid ounces = 175 ml | |
| 1 cup = 8 fluid ounces = 250 ml | |
| 2 cups = 1 pint = 500 ml | |
| 1 quart = 1 litre | |